These Are Strange Times, My Dear

ALSO BY WENDY WILLIS

A Long Late Pledge
Blood Sisters of the Republic

These Are Strange Times, My Dear

Field Notes from the Republic

WENDY WILLIS

COUNTERPOINT
Berkeley, California

These Are Strange Times, My Dear

Library of Congress Cataloging-in-Publication Data
Names: Willis, Wendy, 1966– autor.
Title: These are strange times, my dear : field notes from the republic /
    Wendy Willis.
Description: First paperback edition. | Berkeley, California : Counterpoint,
    2019.
Identifiers: LCCN 2018033720 | ISBN 9781640091511
Subjects: LCSH: Political culture—United States. | United States—Politics
    and government—21st century. | United States—Social conditions—21st
    century.
Classification: LCC JK1726 .W56 2019 | DDC 306.20973—dc23
LC record available at https://lccn.loc.gov/2018033720

Cover design by Sarah Brody
Book design by Jordan Koluch

COUNTERPOINT
2560 Ninth Street, Suite 318
Berkeley, CA 94710
www.counterpointpress.com

Printed in the United States of America
Distributed by Publishers Group West

10 9 8 7 6 5 4 3 2 1

For the citizens of the Crow's Nest—
David, Ruby, Violet & Luke

CONTENTS

A Gnostic Bill of Rights

Becoming Citizen

Ferlinghetti's Perfume

These Are Strange Times, My Dear

———————————

Introduction

SOME DAYS IT SEEMS OUR DEMOCRACY IS SO FRAGILE that if I look at it too hard, it will shatter. Or I will. And it's not just me. Or us. For twelve consecutive years, the Freedom House Index has marked a decline in global freedom. Only a third of American millennials say it is "essential to live in a democracy." A recent study shows early warning signs of what they are calling "democratic deconsolidation" among liberal democracies across the world.

I must ask myself, of course, Why do I care to the point of trembling? To the point of shattering? If the rest of world is moving on from democracy, why shouldn't I? Why can't I? I suspect that's what I am asking myself, over and over, throughout these essays.

In fact, I didn't know I was writing a collection of essays at all until the last year or so. I did know that there were occasions when I wanted to make something other than a poem, that there were times when I wanted to be able to loosen the reins a little or to announce clearly the road I was trotting down. Given what I fret over day in and day out, I guess it's not surprising that I looked for a little more riding room to consider democracy, to consider citizenship.

And what a time it was to search for what Walt Whitman called "the password primeval, the sign of democracy." Over the years I was working on this book, we—and here I mean relatively comfortable white American progressives—escalated from a sort of low-level grumbling about the state of things to a full-throated holler of despair and horror. Looking back, there were warning signs of the eruption that was the 2016 election, but even so, I didn't see it coming. Now, I am not sure if a Trump administration is better or worse than I thought it would be. All I can say is: *It's bad.* And yet I am not one to proclaim that Donald Trump is the most racist, immoral, craven American ever to hold the office of the presidency. After all, he has competition like Andrew Jackson and James Buchanan. I am also not one to proclaim that it can't get worse. Because surely it can. But it has been a bone-rattling shock for those of us who grew up awash in the vague Enlightenment promise that *things get better.* And lately, it sure seems like things are hurtling in the other direction.

But I don't think the problem primarily resides at 1600 Pennsylvania Avenue or even down the street at the U.S. Capitol Building. And it didn't begin in November 2016, either.

This country started off on a nasty festering foot given that most of the land was stolen and that it was cultivated and built by the labor of enslaved people. And given that women didn't have the vote until well into the last century. And given that even now, there is not an insignificant number of Americans who think that the country was better off when people of color and women of all races and gay people and Jews and immigrants and Muslims just knew their place.

There is a lot to worry about. Huge forces are at work, forces greedy for money and power and influence. We are confronted with cataclysm everywhere we look: global climate catastrophe, nuclear proliferation, massive concentration of wealth, genocides, hundreds of thousands of people uprooted by civil war. And it is incumbent on us not to look away.

But there are so many small heartbreaks among us, as well. There is daily and ordinary suffering and cruelty and disappointment. There are individual struggles and midnight terrors. There is despair. And yet there are also hundreds—millions—of acts of kindness and redemption and grace. There is companionship. There is joy. As I wrote these pieces, I couldn't help but be reminded of the words of the poet and essayist Adrienne Rich: "No person, trying to take responsibility for her or his identity, should have to be so alone. There must be those among whom we can sit down and weep, and still be counted as warriors."

That is where I find myself a lot of the time now, wondering about the personal call of citizenship. About the private catastrophes and closely held griefs. I find myself asking about the inner requirements of fierce and ethical citizenship without denying fear and failure, heartbreak and anguish. Dietrich Bonhoeffer—the German theologian executed by the Nazis for his part in the resistance—wrote about "costly grace," which must be sought "again and again." He contrasted it with cheap grace, which is "sold on the market like cheapjacks" and "thrown away at cut prices." Costly grace requires sinners—in Bonhoeffer's view, all of us—to knock at the door over and over. Though Bonhoeffer's call is a little severe, I am attracted to a secular, civic form of that grace-seeking that does not allow for certainty and easy answers. If we are to revivify our souls as citizens, an exacting grace does not allow us to simply adopt and repeat what we hear from our own political tribe. It also doesn't allow us to indulge in pat responses to tangled and barbed moral questions. We must examine our culpabilities, our habits, our cruelties, and then decide what is required of us. We must pursue what Holocaust survivor and moral philosopher Viktor Frankl called an "intensification of the inner life."

Fortunately, we have poets and artists and musicians as companions while we wrestle with these particular angels. Throughout the writing of these essays, I found myself turning again and again to the artists who are holding up a lantern in the dark, who are casting small flickers of light on the path toward a deeper inner life and—in turn—toward a more truthful and empathetic and humane citizenship.

These essays, in their fits and starts, document an era in a small life, one filled with domestic details and the flotsam of the ordinary. And of course, they are also enmeshed in unearned privilege—born of race, of class, of education.

Recently, going back to some of the earlier essays was like paging through the family photo album: *Ah, look how young we all were then.* As the insanity of the 2016 election and its aftermath has obliterated what I thought I knew, some of my earlier grievances now seem a little quaint. In many of those essays, there were observations of particular events that now could be replaced with later, much more outrageous examples. But in the end, I think it is important to keep the moments intact. I think it is important to see it all of a piece, this era in time, some of it protected by not knowing what is to come. In that sense, it is important for all of us to allow our confusion and curiosity and small revelations to stand as they emerged rather than be annihilated by the next garish outburst. Because if we can predict one thing for certain, there will be another outburst.

As Adrienne Rich called us to remember, this is the place we can weep together and not compromise our fierceness. Because here, there is no shame in protecting what is soft and uncertain and fragile. There is no shame in valuing the inner life. There is no shame in pining for what is gone and fearing what is to come. As we look toward the future, not knowing what is ahead for ourselves, for our neighbors, or for democracy itself, I do find comfort—or maybe something more like lively companionship—in Whitman's sense of the matter. As he says, perhaps democracy is of no account, in and of itself. But perhaps, it is the only "fit and full means, formulater, general caller-forth, trainer, for the million, not for grand material personalities only, but for immortal souls."

April 2018

CHRONICLING THE HISTORY OF THE SIEGE

Chronicling the History of the Siege

A Midwinter's Meditation on Resistance

AT OUR HOUSE, THE HOLIDAY SEASON OFFICIALLY BEGINS the Sunday before Thanksgiving. This past November, as in other years, we gathered together with a few dozen of our friends and their kids and out-of-town visitors and neighbors and other stragglers for a pre-Thanksgiving potluck. We ask everyone to bring a sentimental dish and to be prepared to tell the story behind it. Folks bring everything from corn pudding to pecan pie to whipped cream in a can. We've done it so many years that, at this point, we feel sentimental about other families' casseroles. We laugh and overeat and gird ourselves for the family gatherings that are to come, ones that can be full of tight-jawed smiles, hiding out in the kitchen, defensive drinking, or even raised voices and slammed doors.

Presidential election years can be particularly fraught. But our little gathering is pretty politically homogeneous—or I guess it would be more correct to say that the disputes that do break out tend to erupt in the way they do among members of the same team, over purity and competitive righteousness—so it is a relatively safe harbor before heading into the choppy water between Thanksgiving and Valentine's Day.

This past year, many of us hadn't seen each other since the election. So, predictably, every single conversation circled around and eventually landed on fretting over the emergence and soon-to-be inauguration of Donald Trump as the forty-fifth president of the United States. It was an exhausting but seemingly necessary ritual, repeated over and over throughout the evening.

As always, somewhere between the stuffing and the pumpkin pie, my husband and I stood together in the archway that connects the living room and dining room for the toast. He raised his glass and sang out: "Welcome to the headquarters of the resistance."

There were laughs, kisses, and a hearty round of clinking glasses. But in truth, the resistance was everywhere. Seemingly spontaneously, the word that burst forth after the election was "resist." Resist racism and xenophobia. Resist normalizing sexual violence. Resist fascism. And autocracy. Resist the hair. And enmity toward ideas. Resist fake news. Resist platitudes. Resist habitual and pathological lying. Resist propaganda and lack of curiosity and booklessness. Resist idiocy. Resist the id. Resist erupting ugliness, in ourselves and in our country.

And it's not just me and my particular band of writers and

artists and idealistic democracy activists in deep blue 97214. Everywhere I turn, people are writing articles like "Ten Ways to Resist the Trump Administration" or printing T-shirts featuring photos of Princess Leia on the front and "A Woman's Place Is in the Resistance" on the back. Some of the bumper stickers and hoodies are funny, but more than a few of the advice pieces are pious and self-satisfied. Some are dripping with apocalyptic dread. And some are damn useful—like the "Indivisible Guide" informed by the pragmatic political chops of former congressional staffers.

But in the moments when I can calm my limbic system enough to reflect even a little, I wonder how we collectively settled on "resistance" as our rallying cry for opposing Trump and the bigotry and cynicism and narcissism he embodies.

I mean, in some ways, that suits me fine. In fact, I think it is fair to say that I am an expert resister, particularly to the extent that resistance is a kissing cousin of both judgmentalism and naysayerism, which happen to be two of my specialties.

And yet that doesn't quite capture all of what we are called to in this moment. When I finally got up in the wee hours of November 9, 2016, after a few hours in bed—most of them spent shaking and weeping—I made a pot of coffee and sat staring into the fireplace. Then I thought: *I wish I read Polish.* It was an odd thought, but one I could trace. I've long held dear the work of Czeslaw Milosz and his singular blend of the interior and the political, of the sensual and the civic. I love him for his particular form of art-making out of collective heartbreak. And I adore Adam Zagajewski, whose poem "Try to Praise the Mutilated World"—published in the *New Yorker* the week after 9/11—became a sort of holy chant during those wrenching days:

You've seen the refugees heading nowhere,
you've heard the executioners sing joyfully.
You should praise the mutilated world.

And, in early November, as I wondered what I could possibly do in the face of what seemed like certain doom, I could not help but recall the opening lines of Zbigniew Herbert's "Report from the Besieged City":

Too old to carry arms and fight like the others—
they graciously gave me the inferior role of chronicler
I record—I don't know for whom—the history of the siege

There is some comfort in that possibility for a middle-aged mother and writer. At this stage, I am much better suited to the role of chronicler than I am to street fighter. That is not to suggest that there is no room for direct action, even for me. There is and there will continue to be. In between drafts of this essay, I am knitting pussy hats for my daughters and me to wear to the Women's March. I have called and written my members of Congress. I am attending the Writers Resist event in New York next weekend. In fact, I had very seriously considered giving up my law license in 2017 since I haven't been anywhere near a courtroom in almost five years, but given that I have no idea who among my friends might end up in the hoosegow, I think I'd better keep it.

And even as we react to each new horror, I sense there is something else bubbling up from the underground, from the deep unconscious, from the spring beneath the well. But in this agitated state, I can see only glimpses out of the corner of my eye, a whiff of smoke as I rush from one media-fueled panic to the next. I hardly wrote any poems during the fall or early winter. On the one hand, I could argue that I was too busy, that my schedule was full of driving kids to choir concerts and packing lunches and sitting through breakfast meetings. It was. But it was something else, too. Too much Twitter, too little prayer. Too little silence. Too little staring out the window. Too much fast-twitch muscle, too little slow. Too much cortisol. Too much adrenaline. Too much multitasking. Too much minute-by-minute side-eyeing of the train wreck. Too much hand-wringing. Too much outrage and puffed-up righteousness.

That kind of constant, stimulated, externalized anxiety messes with the body and erodes the imagination and the soul. Yesterday, I was doing what I do now—scrolling through Twitter—and there I found essayist Sven Birkerts quoting (naturally) Zagajewski:

> I haven't written a single poem
> in months.
> I've lived humbly, reading the paper,
> pondering the riddle of power

Of course, I retweeted it, but it also shook me into a stark realization. Not only have I written only one poem since the election, but I have stopped thinking in metaphor. My emotional life is ragged, and my mind is full of the words and images generated by Donald Trump, Kellyanne Conway, and Steve Bannon. My vocabulary is stoked by fear and outrage, and my imagination is almost entirely reactive. And the result of constant exposure to all those big, obliterating emotions—the ones perfectly designed to save us from fast and sharp-clawed predators—is that we can't hear the smaller messages, feel the tiny twitch of our littlest finger, discern the scent on the wind as it changes direction. And in that, we lose something. We lose the subtleties of the lateral imagination. We lose access to the whispery voice of something quieter, something deeper.

What does it even mean to resist? It is a mighty thing to say no. To dig in our heels and not allow ourselves to be pulled into some kind of craven worldview constructed by reality television. I think of my dog approaching the front door of the groomer. Of me pulling her leash from the front, her dropping her center of gravity and somehow doubling her weight as she backs away from me. I think of not letting go of the rope in the field day tug-of-war. I will not be pulled across that line. I will not agree to a Muslim ban or roundups of immigrants or a gutting of the Clean Water Act or the hollowing out of public education or an asinine $20 billion wall. I will not be pulled into your swamp of money and ego and xenophobia.

But I think we should consider the possibility that the election itself was also a huge bellowed "no." No pluralism. No globalism. No marriage equality. No other God. No smarty liberals with their fancy degrees looking down on people who work for a living. No black guy elected president. No confusion over who is a man and who is a woman. No sharing the wealth that flows only upstream. No questioning whether three thousand square feet and two semi-new cars is attainable or even desirable, let alone sustainable. No. No. No.

Now—from my ideological corner of the Republic—we are primed to respond with our own colossal rebounding "no." And as much I think it is good and right to do so, I must admit that I do not want my children and grandchildren and great-grandchildren to live in a world in which we careen from one earth-shattering no to the next. I have to believe that no—without any upward energy toward yes—is a downward spiral to more fear, more suspicion, more cynicism and cruelty.

So while we engage in triage resistance, which is righteous and necessary, I wonder what a side-by-side version of life-giving resistance might look like, what bulbs and seeds we might plant and tend so that—soon—we might see some green shoots of yes.

What about resistance as it is thought of in epidemiology? What about disease resistance? What about avoiding getting sick in the first place, inoculating ourselves with practices and habits that make us resilient to even the worst pathogens? I wonder what 2016 would have looked like if we had seen restless populism and media-baiting and televised bigotry as the contagions they were. What then would we have done to shore ourselves up, personally and collectively? What public health strategies would we have deployed before we descended into a full-blown epidemic of rancor and coarseness and open disregard for human dignity, science, and facts themselves? I like to think that we could have taken life-giving steps that would have made all of us more vital and existentially resistant to tyranny and adrenaline-fueled bigotry. Maybe we still can.

In this, I am heartened and inspired by the thinking of the Czech writer, dissident, and eventual president Václav Havel. In 1978, he wrote the widely circulated essay "The Power of Powerlessness," offering both encouragement and a philosophical framework for dissidents throughout the communist bloc. The central point of the essay is that individuals can blow on the dying ember of liberty in a totalitarian regime by "living in truth."

Another way to frame Havel's argument is to think of it as "living in integrity," as living so that our external acts match our internal values. For me, the most radical and life-giving aspect of Havel's thinking is that it de-centers the nasty, repressive regime and re-centers the creative inner lives of the citizens. As he puts it: "There is something negative about the notion of an 'opposition.' People . . . relate themselves specifically to the power that rules society and through it, define themselves, deriving their own position from the position of the regime." But for people who have decided to live their lives in integrity and to follow their own values, it should be framed in a positive light, as defined by their own consciences. Again, Havel:

> For people who have simply decided to live within the truth, to say aloud what they think, to express their solidarity with their fellow citizens, to create as they want and simply to live in harmony with their better self, it is naturally disagreeable to feel required to define their own original and positive position negatively, in terms of something else, and to think of themselves primarily as people who are against something, not simply as people who are what they are.

This is a kind of life-giving resistance I am attracted to and feel compelled to nurture and support when I find it. But it requires careful attention to the inner state, moral examination, and a wide-open imagination. And when that inner work flowers in the outside world, it can be vivid and joyful. I think of the beauty, centeredness, and stamina displayed by the Water Protectors at Standing Rock. And the crazy celebratory spectacle of the Blockadia activists dangling from the St. Johns Bridge—streamers flying—in my hometown of Portland a couple of summers ago. Though they knew that Shell's icebreaker, the *Fennica*, would ultimately leave the port and sail toward the Arctic, the bridge-danglers, the kayakers, and the musicians brought spirit and light to the cause. They were radiant descendants of the folks who quietly conducted sit-ins at lunch counters and pray-ins at white churches and wade-ins at segregated pools during the civil rights movement.

And there are other, less overtly political expressions that spring from living in truth—there are concerts and poems and potluck gatherings. There are satiric monologues and dance mobs and hundreds of thousands of individual acts of kindness and empathy.

As I write this, we are between snowstorms. We began the day yesterday with big feathery flakes falling on top of a few inches of snow and ice, bringing my usually temperate city to near stillness until the afternoon melt. We are awaiting several more inches tonight among the prayers of schoolchildren and introverts. Snow days feel like hours stolen out of time, calling for soup and snowball fights and brandy. But in that anticipatory space, where the world is still chugging but holding its breath, I saw a Facebook photo posted by a friend whose husband jerry-rigged their hummingbird feeder with a shop lamp to keep the nectar from freezing during these cold days. She snapped the photo just as a tiny hummingbird with a bright green chest lit on the red plastic rim of the feeder. It was so tender and creaturely. So companionable. It sent me running for my fat hardback edition of Pablo Neruda's collected odes in search of his "Ode to the Hummingbird," which starts here:

To the colibri,
winged
liquid spark,
a shimmering drop
of America's
fire

And ends here:

Seed
of sunlight,
feathered
fire,
smallest
flying
flag,
petal of silenced peoples,
syllable
of buried blood,
feathered crest
of our ancient
subterranean
heart.

That's right, isn't it? Heating the sugar water for the tiny creatures in the yard is both saying no to that which is cruel and cynical and saying yes to that which is tender and vulnerable and overlooked. That is paying attention. That is care into action. That is the opposite of flashiness, of boastfulness, of one "no" crashing into the next. That is living in truth. That is tending to a shimmering drop of America. That is the resistance.

January 2017

Living Among the Things

On Civic Loneliness

What did I know, what did I know
of love's austere and lonely offices?

—ROBERT HAYDEN

WHEN WE IMAGINE LONELINESS—OR AT LEAST WHEN I imagine it—I think of an elderly woman, a widow maybe, living alone in her one-bedroom apartment, nibbling on her baked potato and waiting for Sunday afternoon when her son will call. I imagine her washing her dish, reading for a few minutes, and turning off the light as one day folds into the next. It is a sad, individual fate that I—being a woman of a certain age—wish and hope to avoid by being especially kind to my children.

As it turns out, though, loneliness is both broader and deeper than my imagined version of the widow with the too-busy and far-flung family. Apparently, loneliness is the new sitting, which for a few months was the new smoking. According to recent reports, social isolation and loneliness increase mortality at about the same rate as fifteen cigarettes a day. And loneliness is about twice as dangerous to our health as obesity. Social isolation impairs immune function and boosts inflammation, contributing to a whole host of illnesses, including arthritis, diabetes, and heart disease.

Loneliness and isolation have consequences for the young and vital as well. We know that teenagers—who are the test subjects for such questions—feel loneliness in direct proportion to the amount of time they spend on social media. It turns out that socializing online gives us a quick hit of connection and a brief sense of well-being, which then rapidly dissipate, leaving us feeling unsatisfied and left out. And consider this: The war correspondent Sebastian Junger, in his book *Tribe*, argues that returning soldiers suffer at least as much from the transition out of a purposeful, highly connected society as they do from exposure to combat. In other words, reentry into the individualism and disconnection of ordinary American society is nearly as traumatizing as war itself.

This is, of course, complicated by colonialism and other forms of large-scale displacement piled on top of economic instability and an ethos of middle-class mobility. Because of all those forms of uprooting, social ties are frayed and sometimes entirely torn, making it difficult for many—if not most—people to find long-term, meaningful relationships outside the immediate family. In fact, nearly half of all Americans report that they are lonely, double the number of those who reported being lonely thirty years ago.

As for me, by all external measures, I couldn't possibly be lonely. I live in a lively household with a husband and busy kids and friendly dogs. I talk to my mother nearly every day. I talk to my sister several times a week. We have a standing Sunday-night dinner with whoever is around, related by blood or choice. I can count eight, maybe ten, friends whom I can call and spill it to, and I have colleagues whom I adore.

And yet I am still nagged by a sort of hollowness that—if it is not true loneliness—is a longing that bears some relationship to loneliness. It is a tickle in the back of the mind, a little ice in the belly.

I suspect that it—whatever this hollowness might be—is related in some way to missing. And that *is* something I can recognize and name. In fact, I think the human activity that I engage in above all others is missing. Many of my aunts and uncles and cousins live in other cities, so I miss them. And my kids are at school all day, so I miss them. And one of my closest friends lives in Alaska, so I miss her. And my best friend has gone on vacation to the redwoods or to some treehouse in southern Oregon or to some fool place she says makes her feel like a hippie or an Ewok. I miss her, too.

Every single day of my life, I miss my grandmother. She died sixteen years ago, and I'm still a little mad that she didn't stick around to meet our youngest daughter. But I miss my grandfather, too, though he died when I was three. I can scarcely remember what he looked like, but the smell of a pipe fills my throat with tears.

I still miss my colleagues from all my prior jobs—City Club

and the Federal Defender's Office and Energy III, the insulation company where I worked the summer after high school. I miss my friends from law school and college and kindergarten. I miss Rodney, the boy who died in a car crash when we were in fourth grade.

In fact, sometimes I miss the people I am with because I am thinking about the fact that they will grow up and go to college or get a different job or go to the grocery store without me. As I drive my daughters to school, I often think, *I miss you even though you are still here.* Sometimes I even say that out loud, but they look at me like they are concerned about my health.

I also miss people I barely know—like the friendly barista who started working in the coffee shop around the corner last winter but who doesn't seem to be there anymore. And all the dogs I've ever had—Zeke and Kaikatsu and Katie and Romeo and Bailey. And Kia, the German shepherd we boarded for two weeks when I was in second grade.

I miss restaurants and coffee shops where I ate and argued and laughed with friends and lovers and kids—Ron Paul on Broadway (and boy, do I miss Ron himself) and Chance of Rain and especially Esparza's, where we went for chicken-fried steak on Thursday nights even though I am a vegetarian.

I miss my uncle Eldon and my great-grandfather Harry, neither of whom I ever met. I miss my cat even though I have never had a cat and I don't see a way in which I will ever have one. But I know that if I did have a cat, his name would be Diego Rivera and he would be a calico, and he would have a gray eye patch. I miss him.

All this missing is a source of conflict between my husband and me, though I didn't know it until recently. After being together ten years, he told me the other day that it bugs him when I say "I'm going to miss you" when he leaves on a trip or when I text "Miss you already" as he drives off to work. It makes him feel bad, like he is doing something to me when he's really just going about his life. I was floored. Maybe mostly because it seems odd that I would not know that something I do virtually every day drives him bat-shit crazy.

But despite my new resolution to keep my missing to myself, missing is actually central to my personality. Because it is all so ephemeral. I know it will be gone. And that makes me miss it—all of it—even in advance. Near the end of Wendell Berry's great novel of loneliness, *Jayber Crow*, Jayber says:

> I whisper over to myself the way of loss, the names of the dead. One by one, we lose our loved ones, our friends, our powers of work and pleasure, our landmarks, the days of our allotted time. One by one, the way we lose them, they return to us and are treasured up in our hearts.

That's it, isn't it? It is not that I am alone in any real way. It's that I am temporary. And so are my parents. And my husband. And—God forbid—so are my children. And so is the bright sun shattering over the trees right now. And the cut lilacs I arranged in the heavy crystal vase I received at a wedding shower before my first marriage. And so is the dog who heard me start to weep at the anticipated loss of it all and jumped out of the chair where she was sleeping to put her head in my lap.

I remember a few years ago when Pat Robertson of *700 Club* fame advised a caller to rebuke any potentially evil spirits that might attach themselves to thrift store purchases. And though he was soundly ridiculed by the secular humanists with whom I keep company, I sort of got it. That's actually one of the things I love about secondhand stores and junk shops. We can find not only bargains but also the shimmering of other lives. There is a connection between what was and what is. This pan that browned the rushed morning pancakes for some other children. This sweater that was pulled on some winter night before I was born. This dress laid neatly across a bed alongside silk stockings in anticipation of a long-awaited dance.

I am reminded of the German American poet Lisel Mueller's poem "Things," which begins:

What happened is, we grew lonely
living among the things,
so we gave the clock a face,
the chair a back,
the table four stout legs

Though I love that poem and its ending ("we gave the country a heart / the storm an eye / the cave a mouth / so we could pass into safety"), I don't feel like I need the objects to be humanized for them to be good company. I am just glad to have them nearby and familiar.

As I sort through all this, I can't stop thinking about an expression that I first heard mentioned by the Potawatomi botanist and writer Robin Wall Kimmerer—"species loneliness." Even from the first moment I read it, I shivered with recognition, though I didn't know precisely what she meant by it. But according to Kimmerer, it is "a deep, unnamed sadness stemming from estrangement from the rest of Creation, from the loss of relationship. As our human dominance of the world has grown, we have become more isolated, more lonely when we can no longer call out to our neighbors."

That sounds right as I rush hither and yon from breakfast dishes to school drop-off to work to the grocery store to homework to bed. Though fresh air keeps me somewhat proximate to sane, there are days when I wouldn't be able to accurately describe the weather if asked. While I know the names and dispositions of the plants and animals in my house and yard, it is a cramped circle. I don't know most of the creatures that live in the park right across the street or in my immediate neighbors' yards. Sure, I know the charismatic ones—the raccoons and squirrels, the purple azalea and the ethereal dogwood. I know the persimmon and the Japanese maple. I pray to spot the coyote that others keep seeing right around us. But there is a lot of indeterminate plant matter and many, many tiny dull birds (the type a South African friend calls "LBJs"—little brown jobs) that I don't know by name. Even as I write it, I realize how disrespectful that is.

Across the street, there are the six huge fir trees that must be from the nineteenth-century dairy farm that sat on the site that is now Laurelhurst Park. But they are so tall that they are only trunks in my line of sight except when I walk home from the south and can see the full height of them towering over the park and our house. Mostly I don't notice them. And there is the grand old maple pushing up the sidewalk in front of our porch. We call it "Ruby's tree," not only because her bedroom windows look out into its branches but also because it seems clear to all of us—including Ruby—that the tree is a particular protector for her during the hard and confusing years of growing up a sensitive girl in this country. I love that tree and—when I remember—implore it to keep up the good work watching over the girl I fear for every waking hour. But ours is a one-sided relationship—one more like the relationship between guardian angel and hapless mortal than a reciprocal one between sentient beings who share the planet at the same time.

One of the only times I have had direct communication—in English—with a plant was in Los Angeles, of all places. It was a Sunday in early June, and my co-workers had just picked me up after an early-morning flight between Portland and LAX. As we drove down an uncharacteristically empty but wide boulevard, I blurted out to my friends: "Look at the flowering chestnuts!" In my head, a clear correction: *Jacarandas, you idiot!* "I mean, jacarandas," I muttered to the car. I am not sure I had ever even heard of a jacaranda at that point, but I looked them up as soon as I was reunited with my computer. And yes, jacarandas they were. That seems a bit more like a reciprocal relationship, revealing to me that such things are possible. But it's never happened again, no doubt because of my distraction and lack of fluency in what is being communicated all around me.

All this gives me pause for what it means to run a society—much less a representative democracy—when almost half of its citizens are lonely and when many of us are disconnected from nearly all nonhuman life. It makes me wonder about our capacity to connect with one another to do the gritty and sometimes rough-and-tumble work of coming together to discuss and then solve the problems facing our communities and our nation. It makes me wonder about our ability—and our will—to effectively steward the planet now that we have taken over nearly every square inch.

I can't stop thinking about the cautions offered by the ever-relevant German theorist Hannah Arendt. Apparently—for some obvious reasons—her 1951 book, *The Origins of Totalitarianism*, is once again in high demand. But beyond her alarming descriptions of 1930s Germany, Arendt also helps clarify how loneliness might have implications for self-governance and democratic society-building. She distinguishes between solitude and isolation and loneliness. Solitude is essentially a fact. In order to think and discern clearly and well, we must do it alone, inside the confines of our own minds, and then check our thinking against the ideas of others when we reenter the social realm. Isolation, however, is a political condition in the sense that people who are isolated from one another cannot or will not work together to create something in their shared interest, nor can they organize to resist tyranny.

But loneliness is another matter altogether. It is existential and is a precondition not just to tyranny but to totalitarianism. As Arendt puts it:

> Totalitarian domination as a form of government is new in that it is not content with this isolation and destroys private life as well. It bases itself on loneliness, on the experience of not belonging to the world at all, which is among the most radical and desperate experiences of man.

Arendt contends that loneliness not only undermines our capacity for collective action—as isolation does—but it also destabilizes our sense of self in a way that makes us vulnerable to the clarity and certainty of radical ideology and totalitarianism.

I wonder about that. While I am in full agreement about

isolation—dividing white poor folks from black poor folks and city laborers from farmworkers is a time-tested political strategy to consolidate wealth, influence, and power in the hands of the already mighty—I have some qualms about her characterization of loneliness.

Of course, I don't want elderly women—or men, for that matter—to be alone in apartments for weeks at a time or for people to have no one with whom to discuss important matters. And I fully agree with the *Guardian*'s George Monbiot when he argues that the individualistic values of late capitalism and neoliberalism are crushing us. As he puts it: "Human beings, the ultrasocial mammals, whose brains are wired to respond to other people, are being peeled apart. . . . Though our wellbeing is inextricably linked to the lives of others, everywhere we are told that we will prosper through competitive self-interest and extreme individualism."

And yet there are ways in which I feel deeply protective of my own loneliness. I don't want to give up the core of my aloneness. I don't think the loneliness I guard is driven by competitiveness, though I know I fall prey to it on occasion. But by staying awake to the fact that all these nearby people and creatures and objects and moments will pass, paradoxically, I am more able and inclined to cherish the company I keep. And I would not want to give up the aloneness of the inner life, the secret life, the one where I ponder the most idiosyncratic and fantastical aspects of my short existence.

So here is where I part ways—or maybe I do—with Arendt. Perhaps it is not loneliness itself that makes us susceptible to totalitarianism—for surely an honest sense of our temporariness and fealty to the inner world strengthens our resolve to live well and with integrity—but perhaps what weakens us is our belief that we are alone in our loneliness.

Everything broadcast and podcast and advertised in our direction suggests that everyone else has it together. That they are out living harmoniously and permanently with their beautiful white-toothed spouses. That they are not lying in bed staring at a blank ceiling feeling the full weight of what it means to have hurt someone they love or wallowing in the dread of an anticipated call from the doctor. That they are not schlumping around their kitchen in their sweatpants, eating canned soup over the sink and worrying about where their children are.

Psychologists report that people are more likely to tell physicians they are depressed than they are to admit that they are lonely. There is shame in loneliness, particularly as we judge the state of our interior lives by comparing them to the carefully curated versions of other people's exterior ones. Perhaps that is what makes us susceptible to a rapacious market, as we seek consumer solutions to existential suffering. And this is where I circle back to Arendt—maybe it is that we cannot admit our aloneness and fears and weaknesses to one another, so we become separated and vulnerable to inflated and facially ridiculous promises made by hucksters, would-be tyrants, and peddlers of fake news.

I guess the questions that leaves us with, then, are these: Are we mature enough as a society to sit together in the missing and the melancholy? Can we take midnight comfort from knowing that our neighbors near and far are also muddling through their days and the loneliness that consciousness brings? Are we a grown-up-enough country to recognize the distraction of political and economic sound and fury for what it is and reclaim togetherness even in our confusion and aloneness? Are we willing to be silent and flexible enough to find kinship in the plants and animals and objects that surround us?

If we are vulnerable enough and brave enough to meet one another there, to admit that we are all suffering the same pangs of missing and impermanence, maybe—paradoxically—we will find the company we are looking for. And not feel so alone.

June 2017

A Million People
on One String

Big Data and the Poetic Imagination

THESE DAYS, IT'S ALL BIG DATA ALL THE TIME. OVER THE past few months, I've seen headlines ranging from "Big Data or Big Brother?" to "Big Data's Little Brother" to "Big Data at the Oscars." Just today I was solicited for a webinar entitled "Big Data Is a Big Deal!" (exclamation point theirs). As Duke psychologist and behavioral economist Dan Ariely recently quipped on his Facebook page, "Big data is like teenage sex: everyone talks about it, nobody knows how to do it, everyone thinks everyone else is doing it, so everyone claims they are doing it."

But the big data debate is not entirely made up of cutesy wordplay. Ever since Edward Snowden first started leaking information about the massive U.S. government spying operation, Americans—for the first time in over a decade—started kicking up some real, honest-to-goodness dust about whether the government can do whatever it pleases if it claims to be protecting us from terrorists. And then there's the "creepy" index that seems to be the new—if somewhat ephemeral—standard for just how far the masters of the internet should be allowed to go in keeping tabs on us. Google's former CEO and executive chairman Eric Schmidt once said that Google's policy was "to get right up to the creepy line and not cross it." Then nearly everyone was creeped out when Target's algorithms knew that a teenager was pregnant before her father did. And when Facebook acquired the virtual reality company Oculus, Minecraft creator Markus Persson said he wouldn't continue to work with Oculus because "Facebook creeps me out." Meanwhile Google's Schmidt argues that online megaretailer Amazon should not be allowed to move ahead with its drone delivery plans because they're creepy.

Even David Byrne—of Talking Heads fame—has gotten into the act, claiming that we should "break up" with the internet, arguing: "The information hoovering that corporations engage in is of a kind with the government surveillance; in both cases we are prey to distant agendas. The three forms (if one includes cyber-crime) of data gathering are all connected—and none of them make us happier or more secure."

But what does big data and its creepy hoovering nimbus of world domination mean for readers and writers of poetry? (And here I use the term "big data" rather loosely, to refer both to *deep* data that records particular individuals' preferences and habits and *broad* data that tracks and amalgamates the activities of vast swaths of the world's population.) I think it's fair to say that as citizens of modernity and—as they call it—"producers of content," poets have a lot at stake in this brave new world. The rules of publishing change on what seems like a weekly basis. Readers and potential readers are barraged with so many words that our poems often feel like tide pools in the path of a tsunami. Copyright protections are ever-moving targets. And for sure, poets have plenty of reason to be concerned when mass government surveillance is the order of the day. Writers and other artists have long been targets for government spying, repression, arrest, and worse.

In 2012, PEN International reported that 878 writers around the world had been arrested by their own governments that year. No fewer than 45 of them were killed and 9 were "disappeared." And need I mention Osip Maldestam, who, in 1934, was arrested and sent to Siberia for privately reading an unflattering poem about Stalin to a group of friends ("His thick fingers are bulky and fat like live-baits / And his accurate words are as heavy as weights. / Cucaracha's moustaches are screaming, / And his boot-tops are shining and gleaming")? Or Ai Weiwei, the Chinese sculptor and filmmaker who was arrested for his work and still lives under a travel ban? So yes, a government that undertakes mass spying on its own citizens should be serious business to the nation's poets and other artists.

It has become all too clear that the internet—with its glittering look-at-me headlines and rat holes and twisty turns—is a culture of temptation. A longing, a desire, a fetish is scarcely felt before it is satisfied in an online world composed of ever-more-sophisticated algorithms. I can have a flicker of an impulse, and within seconds I can connect to a worldwide network formed to save the whales or to reinvigorate public appreciation of the sestina. I can want a new German fountain pen at noon one day and have one delivered to my doorstep by ten the next morning.

But that stunted cycle of longing and satisfaction has its risks. Not only can we find our favorite pens at the lowest cost, but we can also follow our darker and more neurotic impulses, the temptations that real-life social forces usually protect (or at least deter) us from. And I am not just talking about pornography, though one-third of the content on the internet is pornographic, so somebody must be following through on those impulses. When the lawyer or the banker who wants a little extra thrill can stay safely behind the mahogany desk rather than being forced to walk into the peep show with the riffraff, the barriers to temptation are swept away and satisfaction is immediate and private. Or rather, seemingly private.

The internet is the island of the lotus eaters, it is the house of mirrors, it is brothel and donut shop wrapped into one. In fact, the internet in the era of big data is Willy Wonka's chocolate factory, churning out specially designed confections to satisfy our deepest and most compulsive cravings, to play to our weaknesses. For many of us poets, our weaknesses run toward the existential, and the internet, with all its easy connectedness, allows us to quiet—temporarily—the clattering craving for recognition, the desire to be seen. It offers hourly opportunities for poets to come out of the shadows and onto Facebook and Twitter for all to admire. And then we are rewarded—or at least ranked—by the media for our skillful use of Twitter, giving us yet another opportunity to display our Twitter mastery as we retweet the results of the rankings. All this hullabaloo allows us to take our fate into our own hands, to deny market forces, and to push our poems—or more likely our poetic avatars— into the public square whether people are clamoring for them or not. The temptations are many: to flee the loneliness of our individual minds, to short-circuit dull work and self-doubt and wheel-spinning, to trade in the drudgery and mystery of mining the unconscious for quick, self-generated notoriety.

One of the odd things about being a poet in the digital world is the pressure—or the impulse—to display a kind of poetic extroversion, to *be* a poet on the internet. At best, it is a kind of performance: "This is what a poet looks like at her desk, in the laundry room, at the grocery store." At worst, it is an unseemly form of exhibitionism—a kind of poet porn—that drains creative energy out of actually making poems. And all that sharing of poet-ness just feeds information to huge data crunchers that will chomp it up and regurgitate it in some exceptionally persuasive form. Who among us hasn't seen the "Publish Your Poetry Book" banner ad in her newsfeed?

I don't mean to be all pure and holy here. The endorphin hit of that "like" popping up next to the publication update you just posted on your Facebook wall is a neat little thrill for a klatch grown accustomed to being overlooked. Who doesn't want to find an audience for an art that is all too often confined to the university classroom and the indie coffeehouse? But there is something fundamental crumbling beneath us while we banter about the latest gossip of the po-biz. There is some force building that is hostile to the very foundation of poems and the poets who love them. At some basic level, the culture and economics of the internet are rooted in crowdsourcing, in the faith that gigantic quantities of data can and will generate an intelligence that is wiser, cannier, and more prescient than any individual mind. In fact, in 1975, Robert Penn Warren prophetically warned: "The ideal of understanding men and telling their story, noble or vicious, will be replaced by the study of statistics or nonideographic units of an infinite series, and computers will dictate how such units, which do breathe and move, can best be manipulated for their own good. We may not be there yet, but we are on the way."

Few would disagree that we have arrived at the station Warren saw looming down the tracks. Massive quantities of data are used every day to amalgamate, parse, source, predict, and trigger the future. And we have witnessed the internet's considerable potential both for sparking mass collective action (see Arab Spring or the reaction to the Susan G. Komen Foundation's decision to stop funding Planned Parenthood) and for very narrowly targeting and marketing toward individuals, using markers of "type." If, for example, middle-aged, middle-class, white-presenting, urban, college-educated mothers tend to vote for candidates who favor affordable day care and universal sick leave, then people whose internet profiles resemble those women will be microtargeted with political messages focused on issues affecting working mothers. And they will be bombarded with ads for fashionable but comfortable shoes and labor-saving kitchen devices and by news sources focusing on education policy. In fact, I just looked at my Facebook feed and found an ad for the upcoming Summer Camp Expo. (Thanks, Facebook! I've been procrastinating about those summer camps.)

All that attention to the hive mind leaves very little space for the thin reed that is the individual poetic imagination, for the hazy glimpse into the untrammeled interior brought forth by an individual consciousness. As readers and citizens, we have come to rely on poems and poets to anchor us in the inner life, to allow us to overhear a single voice speaking into the melee of modernity. The poet is disruptor, is world-creator and conjurer, and is both guardian and spokesperson for the unconscious. As Wallace Stevens spins out in "The Man with the Blue Guitar":

They said, "You have a blue guitar,
You do not play things as they are."

The man replied, "Things as they are
Are changed upon the blue guitar."

And yet those shimmery-poem-created worlds can evaporate in an instant. On the broad end of the big data spectrum (where individual decisions are consolidated into an undifferentiated mass), the amalgamation of expertise and taste and opinion is a bullhorn for the bell curve, reinforcing the massive majority while obliterating or at least obscuring outliers at either end of the curve. And a lot of times that respect for the majority makes sense. It allows us to serve the most widely held interests, and it exiles loud members of a bigoted minority to their rightful place in the weeds. But let's be honest. Aren't poets and artists often among the outliers (though hopefully not among the bigoted ones)? Aren't we the ones who imagine what isn't but maybe could be? Aren't we the ones often at odds with the big swollen mass in the center? And if that is true, where do outliers fit into the refractive and bloated version of reality that the online world broadcasts back into the culture, reinforcing the broad center of the bell and further marginalizing those who fall on the narrow ends?

In his brilliant little book *Democracy, Culture and the Voice of Poetry*, Robert Pinsky argues that poetry plays an essential role in destabilizing what he calls "mass culture," and the mass that he was responding to was nowhere near as massive as the one we now tap into on an hourly basis. As he characterizes it, mass culture creates a tremendous collective anxiety: "We are simultaneously afraid of constraints making us so much like one another that we will lose something vital in our human nature, and also in fear of becoming so fluently different, so much divided into alien and brutally competitive fragments, gangs or fabricated nationalisms, that we cannot survive."

He argues that poetry is an antidote to both the obliteration and the alienation caused by the dominance of mass culture. As he puts it, "Something deep in poetry operates at the borderland of body and mind, sound and word: double-region of the subtle knot that Donne says makes us man."

But the poetic imagination is a fragile thing, a skitterish thing, and it—like everything else—is being bombarded with sophisticated, made-to-order messages intended to co-opt it for the purposes of retail marketing and political manipulation. And here's where we career into the deep end of the big data spectrum—the segmented isolation that the internet can (and is happy to) generate for us. Moment by moment, we can create an online world that is so singular that it *feels* like an individual mind. It feels like a world created by and for us, a world where our interior life and all its fantasies are made manifest. We conflate our immersion in the online world with the deep space of the imagination because, otherwise, how could it be so connected to our barely felt desires and secret neuroses?

Yet that algorithmically generated experience of deep individuality is synthetic and littered with cookies and tracking code and surveillance cameras. That is not to suggest that without big data, humans are not socially influenced—some would say socially constructed—creatures. We are. But behind the curtain of that digitally generated singularity lurk huge interests amassing power and wealth and that have no fealty to the individual or the rebellious imagination. And further—even if the interests were benign—access to everything all the time (and everything's access to us) obliterates that which is hesitant, nascent, that which sputters before it bursts into being.

By spending time in the depths of the interior without Eric Schmidt or Mark Zuckerberg to guide her, only then does the poet give the poem a chance to approximate that which is most fragilely human, that which is imperfect and flawed but was made by a single mind, unpolished by the "wisdom of the crowd." Again, Stevens speaks to this exquisite imperfection:

> I cannot bring a world quite round,
> Although I patch it as I can.
>
> I sing a hero's head, large eye
> And bearded bronze, but not a man,
>
> Although I patch him as I can
> And reach through him almost to man.

All this is not to argue that the internet is evil or to order the poets back to their garrets with their tallow candles and AOL dial-up. Nor is this intended to suggest that we should return to a world of isolation and unknowingness.

It is to argue, however, that all this connectedness and

knowledge is not free and that we are making trade-offs,
sometimes without thinking very hard about them. It is to argue that we should be more alert, that we should think more
deeply about how we participate in the digital world, and that
there actually should be a trade in the trade-offs. It is to argue
that poets should lead the way toward a more mature relationship with the digitally generated world, one that starts with
our eyes wide open. It is to argue that poets and other artists have a particular stake in speaking out when we see overreaching by governments, by employers, by corporations. It is
to suggest that we poets take a deep breath and think artisti-
cally, intentionally, and strategically before we throw ourselves
wholeheartedly into the work of creating an online brand.
Let's challenge ourselves to resist the temptation to overshare
or reach for the salve of temporary recognition or join the circus of poetic exhibitionism.

But more than all that, it is to suggest—ever so gently—
that it would serve us well to protect our fragile and susceptible
imaginations, to be defensive of their soft animal underbellies.
And if we do, then, just maybe we can safely step into the rush-
ing river that is the internet. Maybe then we can embrace it for
what it is and come and go as we please. Maybe then we can join
the crowd in the way Stevens imagined:

> A million people on one string?
> And all their manner in the thing,
>
> And all their manner, right and wrong,
> And all their manner, weak and strong?

The feelings crazily, craftily call,
Like a buzzing of flies in autumn air,

And that's life, then: things as they are,
This buzzing of the blue guitar.

November 2014

The Night Sits Wherever You Are

On Transparency and Secrets

LAST WEDNESDAY NIGHT, MY MOTHER DID SOMETHING unusual. She called after dinner. She never calls after dinner. "Wendy," she said, "I have stage four metastatic colon cancer." I stared out the window. A few minutes earlier, snow had started to fall and was just beginning to stick to the grass and the sidewalks. My mind skittered and struggled. I had talked to her that morning. And the morning before that. In fact, I talk to her most every morning on my way to work. Just to check in. Never once, in all those conversations between school drop-off and my desk did she ever say she had found a lump in her belly. Or that she felt uncomfortably full or gassy. Never once did she tell me that she was lying awake at night waiting for her doctor to call with life-changing test results.

My heart pounded in my ears, and my imagination careered down the well-worn tracks of catastrophe. The screech of brakes, a siren around the corner, a cough heard from another room are enough to send my brain racing toward death and disaster. Last night, I became a motherless daughter before the first two sentences were out of her mouth. I mostly sat in silence, trying to fight off hysteria.

But then my mom passed the phone to my sister. I burst out in rage. Not at my sister exactly. Not entirely. But I was infuriated that I went from blissful know-nothingness to stage four—incurable—cancer. I called her—and my parents— "secret-keeping idiots," which I'll admit was not my pithiest, or my kindest, comeback. But I felt—and even now that I am calmer, still feel—betrayed by the fact that I was in near-daily contact with my mom and we talked about everything from Donald Trump's proposal to arm teachers to my nephew's interception in last weekend's seven-on-seven football tournament to my daughter's upcoming graduation party, and no one told me about the catastrophic possibilities lurking in the background. My sister said that they didn't want to worry me, then hung up on me after snarling, "There is no conspiracy against you."

This was the second day in a row I had gotten in a spat with a dear one about secrets. The night before, I'd asked my daughters to clear the table after supper. Ruby stood and started to walk away. "Violet will do it." "No," I said. "You need to do it together." They exchanged a flicker of a glance, and Violet jumped up. "I'll do it." "Nice," I snapped to Ruby. "You're blackmailing Violet to keep her secrets." "Mama . . . ," Violet wheedled. They both laughed. Violet cleared the table, and Ruby headed for the couch. I blinked my stinging eyes and stomped upstairs to fold towels.

I try not to make a habit of snarling at the girls, and I haven't had a conversation involving a raised voice with my sister in probably twenty years. But I'm still not comfortable with where either conversation landed. In the case of my sister, I'm sure some of it was just a way to distract myself from terror and grief. If I am outraged because I was left out of some vital conversation, I don't have to focus on the fact that my mother—who is the hub around which the rest of us turn—is facing a life-threatening illness. And with regard to my daughters, I almost immediately started imagining what horrible, dangerous activity Violet could be hiding. I went through the litany—boys, drugs, riding in cars with new drivers who were drunk or high or both. All those things make my stomach churn and my hands and feet turn to ice.

But it goes further than that. I realize I nurse a kind of overall entitlement to know. And it's not just me, either. It's become a cultural obsession, this license to know. Among the unwritten rights we Americans cherish, the right to know seems to be one of the most highly regarded and regularly asserted. We want to know the number of calories in a caramel latte and the ins and outs of celebrity divorces. We want to know our neighbors' opinions of the brake shop down the street and the salary of the person working next to us. We want to know not just the details of our friends' and family members' lives but also the granular comings and goings of virtual strangers.

And it's no different in our political life, either. We expect to know about candidates' policy positions, the details of their relationships with their children, and whether they prefer cats or dogs.

Part of it is that politics—both electoral and governing— have merged with entertainment, and it's as if the two have hybridized into one insatiable mass culture, with no distinctions between those who make decisions about potential nuclear annihilation and those who live in a group house on MTV. Of course, entertainers—as world citizens—are well within their rights to express their opinions about political or social issues in this country or any other. But they have an almost inconceivably powerful amplifier driven by worldwide broadcasts and social media. Meanwhile, White House staffers are being trailed by paparazzi, and we follow who is in and who is out of the president's good graces like we used to follow love triangles on *Days of Our Lives*.

As politics and entertainment merge into a huge conglomerate, we ordinary folks swivel from one mass experience to another, whether it is the Super Bowl or a school shooting or a presidential election. Our sense of what we need to know in order to be informed and functional citizens keeps shifting. And—as a result—our thinking on the question of what we are entitled to know has become muddied and perhaps even a bit untrustworthy.

It is an American bromide that "sunlight is the best disinfectant." While the expression originated with Justice Louis Brandeis in the pages of *Harper's* in 1913, we have distilled it down to what we have come to call "transparency," which we invoke as an unassailable social and democratic good. We talk about the value of transparency in everything from our marriages to our workplaces to the inner machinations of federal agencies.

For sure, the right to know what is in our food and medicine has prevented thousands of unnecessary deaths. And transparency surrounding public contracting and decision-making does a good deal to deter—or at least reveal—corruption. Plus, transparency rules are relatively easy to implement. The day after he was inaugurated, President Obama launched what he called the Open Government Initiative, asserting, "Openness will strengthen our democracy and promote efficiency and effectiveness in government."

Behind this drive for transparency, there is a good-hearted hope that if the public sees government at work, citizens will like it better, will trust it more. They will better understand hard, no-win trade-offs and constrained resources. They will see everybody just struggling to do the right thing, regardless of whether they agree with the outcomes.

But it doesn't quite work that way. In fact, some studies suggest that the citizens who pay the closest attention to the news are the ones who have the most negative feelings about the tone and tenor of politics.

Plus, from a purely tactical perspective, maximum transparency might not incentivize the types of behavior we are looking for in our public officials. By requiring that all the people's business take place in full view of the rest of us, we are asking elected officials and other public agents to be "on" all the time, triggering a whole panoply of performative impulses and suppressing more desirable ones, like listening before talking or sharing the limelight and the credit.

In an unusually fresh look at the 1787 Constitutional Convention, lawyer and scholar Derek Webb argues that part of the reason that the convention was so successful—and so civil—was that most of the debate was off the record. Neither the votes nor the proceedings themselves were officially recorded. Years later, James Madison reflected:

> Opinions were so various and at first so crude that it was necessary they should be long debated before any uniform system of opinion could be formed. Meantime, the minds of the members were changing and much was to be gained by a yielding and accommodating spirit. Had the members committed themselves publicly at first, they would have afterwards supposed consistency required them to retain their ground, whereas by secret discussion, no man felt himself obliged to retain his opinions any longer than he was satisfied of their propriety and truth and was open to argument.

In other words, the opacity of the proceedings allowed the delegates to experiment with ideas, listen, persuade one another, and change their minds. In that sense, lack of transparency boosted and enhanced the potential for creativity and, ultimately, for agreement. When every interaction is observed—and these days, often recorded and broadcast—we create irresistible incentives for performance, posturing, and stubbornness. If the cameras are off and the doors are closed, there is a least some possibility that genuine problem-solving might take place.

It also makes me consider the role of integrity in all this. Here's another well-worn axiom: "Integrity is doing the right thing, even when no one is watching." The problem, though, is that if transparency is our highest public value, there is never a time when no one is watching. It is like the unwinnable cat-and-mouse game we play with teenagers, struggling to watch over them ever more ingeniously, them escaping our snares ever more elegantly, and no one learning to make good choices on their own. Similarly, as we rely more on our own watching and knowing to protect ourselves from public malfeasance, we don't allow ourselves to trust the good judgment, moral code, and integrity of those we elect to represent us. And elected officials know it. In the same way that teenagers often push the limits of their behavior up to the point where they think they might get caught, so—in many cases—do our public officials.

This sets in motion a spiral of false hope and disappointment. We act out a stylized expectation that elected officials—and appointed ones for that matter—should be beyond the weaknesses and foibles that we see in ourselves and our neighbors. We suspect, however, that it's too good to be true, so we keenly watch their every move and then revel in shock and schadenfreude when they make a mistake or behave badly.

We are all implicated in this spiral. The more transparency we demand and become accustomed to, the more we stoke our own appetites for knowing. We come to crave the details of every peccadillo, misstep, or outburst. And then we celebrate the failure with mock horror and—often—banishment from public good graces.

Here, I realize I am on thin ice. For generations, powerful people—mostly men—have successfully maintained a rampart between their public accomplishments and their private transgressions. We have averted our eyes from boorish, abusive, and outright criminal behavior, arguing that we can separate the bad acts from the actor and his otherwise laudable accomplishments. That, of course, needs to stop. And silence, secrecy, and shame are some of the most effective tools used by powerful men to keep racking up successes and accolades while women and other vulnerable people spend time, creative energy, and life force trying to avoid being assaulted or gaslighted or both.

It is the centerpiece of the #MeToo movement that victims of violence and harassment will no longer slip away in silence and shame. They are naming names and telling tales. And god love them for doing it. I know all too well the feeling of watching a man move with ease in the world, advancing in his career and thriving in his family, while I recognize a whole other side to him, one that is stained by a dark insistence in getting what he wants when he wants it, regardless of who it harms.

But there is a cost buried in all this knowing. Now, several months into the #MeToo movement, I find myself feeling poisoned by the steady—and detailed—diet of accounts of sexual violence. This is not to suggest that the victims shouldn't tell their stories, but just that it has implications for all of us to bear witness to the punishing particularities of so much violence and abuse. Here in my own community, a victim recently came forward to tell the story of her sexual assault by two prominent Portland men. The newspaper account was long and relentlessly specific. I know one of the assailants a little, and reading every ugly detail of two men trying to rape a small and very drunk woman still lives in my mind and body and imagination. Good for her for doing what she needs to do. Good for her for speaking up. One of the men—the one I know—had recently filed to run for elected office, and the victim decided she could no longer stand silent. But to be believed, she had to reveal an account so horrifyingly specific that those of us who read the story still carry it around in the rest of our lives—our work lives, our social lives, our sex lives. As a friend said to me recently, "I can't help but take these images home. To my bed. With my wife." And I can't help but be caught in the undertow, which drags me back to the moment when I was eighteen years old and realized: *This man is going to do what he wants regardless of what I say or do*. And which drags me back to years of self-loathing and mistrust and wretchedness.

Even outside the particular painful complexities of this era of reckoning, I find that the relentless need to know is also damaging my ability to discern what is worthy of my attention and what is a sideshow. There are times when I am truly arrested by a detailed telling of another's life—as I was when I read a *Washington Post* account of a Kentucky funeral director who has seen a 75 percent increase in what he calls "deaths of despair"—in a way that sparks empathy and opens a new way of looking at an issue otherwise dominated by trends and statistics. But discernment is clouded by volume and by the ease of following my worst gossipy and prurient impulses.

As I do my morning news scan, details of the Iran nuclear deal merge with the breakup of a congressman's marriage. Yesterday, I read that the atomic Doomsday Clock moved to 11:58 and immediately afterward read a rumor that Melania Trump spends three to four nights a week in a hotel. "Does she go back and forth with a full motorcade?" I wondered. And then I was off into full-blown distraction and speculation. It would take a tremendous amount of self-delusion to argue that knowing all the minute details of Melania Trump's private life makes me a better citizen.

The insistence on knowing also has a subtler and more corrosive effect on what I will dare to call our souls. According to former Google CEO Eric Schmidt, every two days we create as much information as we did from the dawn of civilization up until 2003. Humans are now exposed to as much information in one day as a person in the fifteenth century was in a whole lifetime. That relentlessness is hard on the human organism no matter what the content. But the ecosystem of exhibitionism and voyeurism we find ourselves in now keeps us firmly planted in shock and agitation. It buffets us from one salacious tale to another, leaving us with little capacity to dwell in the inner world or even the quiet of one moment passing to the next.

The inner life is where we hold the inchoate and the fragile, as well as the feared and mysterious. It is the place where we have access to that which is larger—as well as smaller—than our daily obsessions and worries. Jung put it very directly: "Your visions will become clear only when you can look into your own heart. Who looks outside, dreams; who looks inside, awakes." The inner life does not trade in sunlight and revelation; rather, it requires quiet and more than a little dark.

This is where the needs of our souls begin to collide with the public (and, for that matter, private) culture we have created. We tell ourselves—and others—that the only legitimate reason for secrets is that we are trying to conceal something shameful. We say "I don't have anything to hide" or "My life is an open book." And we repeat it as a way to justify our own need-to-know run amok. In another inimitable moment, Eric Schmidt dismissed concerns about Google's privacy policy by saying, "If you have something that you don't want anyone to know, maybe you shouldn't be doing it in the first place."

And yet when we are honest with ourselves, we know there is a place for the unrevealed, for the private, for the secret. There is dignity in the impulse to hold something dear by protecting it from the harsh light of another's gaze. One of the great odes to secrecy is Anton Chekhov's short story "The Lady with the Dog." The heart of the story is an affair between a middle-aged Muscovite banker, Gurov, and a newly married young woman, Anna. After meeting in Yalta, they begin what Gurov believes will be a brief and forgettable affair. But they are both drowning in longing—him for an escape from the doldrums of family life and her for an existence larger than the one she has accepted. They find a spark of promise in each other, and though the story stays famously unresolved, Chekhov says of Gurov:

> He had two lives: one, open, seen and known by all who cared to know, full of relative truth and of relative falsehood, exactly like the lives of his friends and acquaintances; and another life running its course in secret. And through some strange, perhaps accidental, conjunction of circumstances, everything that was essential, of interest and of value to him, everything in which he was sincere and did not deceive himself, everything that made the kernel of his life, was hidden from other people.

It's as if the deep hiddenness of their love—the secrecy of it— was what gave it worth. The "kernel of Gurov's life" was essential not because it was shameful—though that might have been the initial reason for hiding the affair—but because it was sheltered from the casual and mundane glare of the day-to-day.

There is something thrilling about keeping one's own counsel and living—at least some of the time—in the shadows of interiority. But our preoccupation with "daylighting" (what a verb!), while simultaneously narrating everything that is happening to ourselves and everyone else, prevents us from protecting the space or even having the skills to attend to that which is dark or mysterious or nascent.

Besides being shortsighted and narrow-hearted, this approach to our inner lives has serious risks. In 1945, right after the end of the war, Jung warned us against ignoring the shadow:

> Filling the conscious mind with ideal conceptions is a characteristic of Western theosophy, but not the confrontation with the shadow and the world of darkness. One does not become enlightened by imagining figures of light, but by making the darkness conscious.

Jung's theory is that if we acknowledge and work with our shadow side, it is entirely less likely to overtake us. But that takes quiet and interiority and, in some real sense, secrecy. Recognizing that each of us carries the dark as well as the light, Mahmoud Darwish starts his poem "Your Night Is of Lilac" here: "The night sits wherever you are. Your night / is of lilac." He writes later in the poem, "Night / is the covenant of night."

In so many ways, it is easier to stay in the brightness—and the shallowness—of what mythologists call "the middle world." And none of this is to suggest that we should return to an era of secrecy that protects the powerful and crushes the vulnerable. But I do suggest that we ask ourselves whether sometimes we use sunlight to blind us to and distract us from the things we most fear, the things that are most essential.

And I also know that I, at least, need to face up to the reality that—no matter how much I want it to—knowing can't save me from everything. Yes, knowing that mayonnaise can't be left out all night has saved millions from illness and death. And knowing that Harvey Weinstein is a sexual predator has changed the face of Hollywood forever. But knowing has its limits. Knowing the ins and outs of Angelina Jolie's divorce has not made me more empathetic or more gracious. Knowing about every affair of every member of Congress has not made either chamber more likely to do our business efficiently or with integrity. And knowing one day or one hundred days sooner that my mother has incurable cancer will not save her—or me—from crippling worry or from the suffering that most certainly is to come.

March 2018

I Hear the Place That Can't Be Named

One Writer's Reflections on the Right to Be Forgotten

WHOEVER THE SMARTY PANTS IS IN THE EUROPEAN Union who came up with the "right to be forgotten" clearly did not grow up in Springfield, Oregon. I will tell you from recent experience around the Christmas tree that no one's most embarrassing deed is ever—ever—forgotten. Depending on the year, between ham and scalloped potatoes and sugar cookies and gingerbread, we can talk about bad hair and failed businesses and freshly minted divorces and car wrecks and missed jump shots and lost children and a well-placed stink eye from decades—if not centuries—ago. And it's not just Springfield, either. I know my friends from Houston and Toronto and Durban are also deep in gossip that has ossified into mythology, into culture.

And yet I understand the impulse to forge such a shiny new

right, like the right to be forgotten. It sounds unassailable. And so modern. The Europeans are striving to protect the desire of individuals to "determine the development of their [lives] in an autonomous way, without being perpetually or periodically stigmatized as a consequence of a specific action performed in the past." They've been working on it for quite a while. After a few commissions and task forces and passes at legislation, the Court of Justice of the European Union stepped in and concluded that—if requested—search engines must break links to publications about individuals that contain information that is "inaccurate, inadequate, irrelevant or excessive."

In the lead case, a Spanish man sought to have links removed related to an old real estate auction he had participated in to settle a social security debt. He argued—and the court agreed—that links to articles about the auction should be removed from Google "because they infringed his right to privacy—they weren't relevant to his situation today." Of course, late-night comedians had a field day with the fact that no one had ever heard of Mario Costeja González and his bad debts until he made legal history by forcing Google to forget about his troubles with the social security system.

From the moment I first started reading about such a right, I was enchanted. I loved the sound of it, the idea that our most humiliating deeds could be erased, could just be obliterated. Plus it was Europe! So smart and progressive about these things, the Europeans. And because many of the digital privacy warriors I admire were promoting it, I was ready to sign up.

Yes sir, I would love the right to make other humans forget events that by current lights are "inaccurate, inadequate, irrelevant or excessive." That's a superpower I would like to have. In

my family, stories are told and retold dozens—if not hundreds—
of times in exactly the same way, often to prove that I am the
absentminded one, my sister is the practical one, and that it was
glaringly obvious from the moment of our births.

I would love to have family members—dear as they are—
stop telling tales from forty years ago. And I would like others
to forget the years when I dyed my hair the color of genetically
modified corn, making me appear a confusing combination of
forbidding and terrified because my eyebrows created nasty dark
gashes in my otherwise colorless face. And others to forget the
times I cried at work or the horrible night I got drunk at a party
and mocked a friend for her weight just to make myself feel better after a nasty breakup. And still others to forget twenty years
of sloppy overlapping relationships and the trail of cruelties and
wounds left behind. Seriously, it makes me cringe to know that
there are people living on this planet who remember any of those
things. Boy, do I want the right to have them forgotten.

As I look back on all those frailties and failings and just
plain sins, it's a bleeding miracle and incontrovertible proof of
grace that I have any friends and loved ones at all. And it makes
those enduring, scarred, tender bonds of kinship and friendship
among the dearest things in my life. It is remembering and loving anyway—not forgetting—that binds us even if the recollections are absurd, undignified, cruel, or humiliating.

Of course, there are examples of expungement that fall in
their own category. We don't want folks who have served their
time in the criminal justice system to be forever consigned to
harassment and employment discrimination and struggles
to find housing. We don't want victims of revenge porn to be
permanently saddled with the vindictive impulses of creepy

ex-boyfriends. But as for most of the rest of our poor choices, extermination from others' memories seems counter to the human condition and distances us from the acts of forgiveness and generosity that enmesh us in culture and community.

I love this poem by Paul Celan, which reads as if it erupts from rumor and faint memory, passed lip-to-ear over the generations, offering grace and almost mythological solace:

> I hear that the axe has flowered
> I hear that the place can't be named,
>
> I hear that the bread which looks at him
> heals the hanged man,
> the bread baked for him by his wife,
>
> I hear they call life
> our only refuge.

> TR. MICHAEL HAMBURGER

What if the hanged man or his wife or the flowering axe were forgotten in a fit of shame? What if the links were broken? To what would we attach ourselves in our own desperate and flawed search for refuge? How would we find company in our own dark—but equally fleeting—hours?

Besides, we're an untrustworthy species when it comes to memory. It's not just our biological tendency toward forgetfulness, but a collective impulse to flee that which is painful or shameful, that which calls our motives into question. We don't seem to have trouble forgetting land grabs and genocides and lynchings and burnings at the stake and slavery and blankets laced with smallpox. Americans, in particular, aspire to be a forward-looking people. We tell ourselves that we should not dwell in the past but lean into the future, with all its promise of progress and boundless growth. As Carolyn Forché put it in the introduction to her remarkable anthology *Against Forgetting: Twentieth-Century Poetry of Witness*:

> Modernity, as twentieth-century German Jewish philosophers Walter Benjamin and Theodor Adorno argued, is marked by a superstitious worship of oppressive force and by a concomitant reliance on oblivion. Such forgetfulness, they argue, is willful and isolating. It drives wedges between the individual and the collective fate to which he or she is forced to submit.

In Japan, people who survived the atomic bombs at the end of World War II are training younger people to be "memory keepers." The survivors fear that if they do not formally assign their memories to members of the next generation, it will be easier and more convenient to forget the suffering brought on by war as Japan moves away from its postwar commitment to oppose militarism.

There is also the risk that such a right will be exercised most vigorously by those who have the most to gain. I fear the right to be forgotten is less likely to be invoked by some hapless thirty-year-old who doesn't want his boss to see the out-of-focus middle school photos of him smoking weed than by oil spillers and sweatshop owners and prospective candidates for Congress.

And forgetting, after all, has its own vagaries. Lord knows, there are plenty of things I have forgotten I wish I could remember. I can't remember my first kiss or even who it was with. I can't call up the voice of family members whom I miss like a limb. I barely remember my high school graduation or my parents' fortieth wedding anniversary. I don't recall my junior prom. I have forgotten teachers' names and the wallpaper in my childhood bedroom and books that held me rapt for days at a time. And it's getting worse. Not only does middle age bring on an all-out search for nouns, but new research shows that our smart little devices are eroding our ability to store memories. Apparently, the passivity of scrolling through the internet doesn't create the pathways to solid memory like actual embodied human experience does.

It's a lonely thing, forgetting and being forgotten. And most of us will be forgotten someday. For me, that's even more chilling than the memory of my senior picture featuring me leaning up against a fake tree in my pink polo shirt and purple pullover. And I have to ask myself, in the wisps of recall that might remain of me, do I want my descendants to think of me as a carefully curated brand that I control from beyond the grave? Or would I rather them catch a glimpse of *me*, flaws and all?

And what does it mean for our own sense of self if we get to pick and choose our own history? Do *we* also get to forget those times when we were silly or cruel? Or will we still suffer over them, even when the rest of the world has forgotten?

And isn't that what we—as writers and struggling human beings—are doing in this business anyway, fighting against inevitable forgetting? Aren't we struggling to make meaning in the face of imperfection? And even more so, in the face of death? The "right to be forgotten" sounds logical, even beautiful but—like so many other things in this human-dominated age—is willful and pointed toward hubris and destruction. In the same way that I might yearn for "the right to eat gummy bears without my teeth falling out" or "the right to fly if I put a quarter in my shoe" or "the right to leave on every light in the house without burning a lump of coal," there are aspects of the human condition I can't control. Like other people's memory of me. And I guess that is one of the beautiful messes created by being alive in full view of others.

Honestly, it's not that I even care that much if Google breaks its links to news articles from ten years ago—though I suspect those fractures will be strategically employed to bury the misdeeds of the wealthy and the powerful and the sociopathic—it's that I worry that by asserting we have a legally enforceable human right "to be forgotten," we are getting a little too big for our britches. We are—once again—trying to transcend what it means to be imperfect mortals muddling through in the company of other sad-sack mortals. It's about us trying to be superhuman. It's about us asserting our will over the inner lives of others in a desperate attempt to make ourselves feel less broken.

But as those of us from Springfield, Oregon—and every other tight-knit community on the planet—know, we can never run fast enough. It's too late. Our tiny humiliations and poor choices have already been codified into lore that may or may not be passed to the next generation, keeping writers and therapists at full employment for decades to come. Our cruelties and failures are on full display and will be for the foreseeable future, whether Google knows about them or not. And here we all are, linked together, loving each other anyway.

February 2016

Tilt

On Public Outrage

IF BUMPER STICKERS ARE ANY INDICATION, MY PRECINCT in deep blue Portland, Oregon, is one of the world capitals of outrage. There is the simple declarative "If you're not outraged, you're not paying attention" and the sarcastic "Is that true or did you hear it on Fox News?" or the direct "Stop using Jesus as an excuse for being a narrow-minded bigoted asshole!" I suppose there must be a conservative outrage capital as well—maybe Dallas or Jacksonville or Oklahoma City—where SUVs are covered in quips about political correctness and gender-neutral bathrooms and the Second Amendment.

In fact, if—in addition to our geographically and politically sorted bumper stickers—Twitter and cable television and comment sections on news sites are any indicators, outrage seems to be the emotion that dominates all of our political and civic spaces. The left is shouting about Russia and the white nationalists occupying the White House. The right is carrying on about Benghazi and the preciousness of snowflake college students. It appears that our populace is in a perpetual froth with very little room for anything else.

The dictionary definition of "outrage" is "an extremely strong reaction of anger, shock, or indignation." I sort of love that it is derived from Old French, that it comes from *outré*, "to push beyond bounds." That's the "out" part. I do wonder how outrage differs from anger or fury or just plain rage, but I think it has to do with a sort of propelled, externalized anger. That sounds about right in the current political climate.

Truth be told, I'm also kind of in love with my own outrage. It makes me feel less powerless, and it obliterates all those pain-soaked emotions like confusion and heartbreak and grief. By staying high on outrage, I can keep moving at seventy miles an hour and not stop to feel what's really happening.

There is so much suffering and injustice in the world, the only moral response seems to be anger and righteousness followed by proclamations of the overall wrongness of it all. Recently, several of my friends posted and tweeted a photograph of twenty-three-year-old Turkish trans activist Hande Kader, who was raped and murdered; her body, which had been set on fire, was found abandoned in a forest. The photograph that accompanied the story in many of the world's newspapers was of Kader being arrested at a pro-LGBT demonstration last summer. You can see the police officer's hand gripping her upper arm, her face crumpled with tears and terror. That followed the week in which the world saw the photograph of five-year-old Omran

Daqneesh caked in dust and blood after he was rescued from a building that was bombed in Aleppo, Syria. His ten-year-old brother died. His mother was hospitalized. Five other children and three adults were killed in the same airstrike. Eleven million Syrians—more than half the prewar population of the country—have been killed or forced to flee their homes.

Outrageous. All of it. Along with the nation's police officers continuing to shoot unarmed black teenagers. And our craven unwillingness to make even slight lifestyle concessions to slow global climate change despite the fact that 6.9 trillion gallons of rain fell on Louisiana in one week, killing thirteen people and causing $30 million in damage. And the fact that nearly half the world's population lives on less than $2.50 a day while less than 1 percent of the population controls nearly half the world's wealth. Oh, and an animal is abused every ten seconds in this country, with a strong correlation between animal abuse and domestic violence. And last summer, some dude with a suspended license and a gold Lexus hit and killed a teenage girl while he was driving sixty miles per hour down a street in our neighborhood. Yes, there is a lot to be infuriated over. And I am infuriated a lot of the time.

I need to know the names of Omran Daqneesh and Hande Kader and Egyptian poet Shaimaa al-Sabbagh, who was killed by the police while laying a wreath in Tahrir Square. And Tamir Rice and Sandra Bland and Eric Garner and Alton Sterling and Walter Scott. I need to hear the names and stories of Edward Sotomayor and Stanley Almodovar III and Kimberly Morris and Eddie Jamoldroy Justice, who sent his last text from the Orlando Pulse nightclub saying, "Mommy I love you. In club they shooting."

Just writing these names out, I am outraged all over again. And yet I suspect that the world is really no more brutal than it has ever been. We just know about it now. In real time. So of course we're outraged. It at least tells us that we're human. And that we care.

And there's another fully understandable aspect of our outrage, both genuine and performed. It gives us a chance to feel something—and express it—in the public square. Jeffrey M. Berry and Sarah Sobieraj, in their book *The Outrage Industry: Political Opinion Media and the New Incivility*, argue that marketed outrage provides a more human and engaging experience of civic life than the rational cost-benefit analysis we have been sold by the Enlightenment and its devotees. Berry and Sobieraj claim, "It is easy to see why audiences might find their favorite columnists, bloggers, or hosts more entertaining than a conventional commentator. In outrage there is performance. There are jokes. There is drama. There is conflict. There is fervor. There is even comfort, as audiences find their worldviews honored." In other words, there are feelings.

From the time we are tiny children, we are told to be polite, controlled, and calm in public. Anger, grief, joy, disappointment are saved for the family, and usually in palatable doses even there. Nowhere is the rational mind and its companion, dry discourse, more valued than in a discussion of public issues. We are taught to admire and emulate that which is well reasoned, persuasive, and stripped of the corrupting influence of human emotion. And to some extent, that makes sense—we know that fear and bigotry and lust for power lead to bad outcomes. But our devotion to the rational and the dry also asks us to check our whole selves before entering the public arena. We are allowed to bring mind, body, and spirit to our lives as parents and spouses and lovers, and even our lives as consumers, but we are asked to bring only our big frontal lobe and its executive functions to questions of politics and our shared civic life.

That's both impossible and dull. So outrage bubbles up and spills all over our nicely-typed-out pro/con policy arguments. And outrage is often a big, fat dog whistle. It tells us who our people are. If we join in the outrage over, say, a particular Supreme Court decision, it not only makes us feel less powerless in the face of nine old, arcanely educated power brokers in robes but also makes us feel like we belong in some important way: "See, I am nestled in here among the forty-eight people who liked my Facebook post and agree with my opinions. I have friends, community, compatriots."

This issue of publicly expressed outrage is complicated for women. In my distinctly matriarchal upbringing, anger was not one of the tools available. The means by which to express one's opinions and get what one wanted involved off-hand remarks, gossip, and social isolation. A raised voice, a harsh tone, or a direct invective was 100 percent off-limits. We—me along with my mother and sister and grandmother and cousins—are world champions in moves resembling the shrug-off and the whispered "Did you see . . . ?" But for all our accomplishments in indirection, we were not really permitted to express—or even really feel—full-flowered anger. I know that I am not alone in this and that it is even more fraught for African American women and other women of color who are immediately swept into the bin of some nasty stereotype the moment an eyebrow gets arched. (See, for example, the interruption and scolding of Senator Kamala

Harris as she presses witnesses appearing before the Senate Judiciary Committee.)

So, for some of us, our foray into the world of political and social outrage has been liberating and sort of naughty. It feels empowering and validating and sleekly forbidden. And who am I to deny such a feeling?

My love affair with outrage is starting to sour just a bit, however. I have started to feel a little poisoned by my own vitriol, despite the never-ending parade of events to be disgusted over. There is something sort of unhinged about it all, the pouring on of outrage like gas on a tire fire. Sure, the first image that pops into our minds when we think "unhinged public behavior" is Donald Trump, but the left has no space for tsk-tsking on this one. Public castigation is one of our superpowers. Think Rachel Dolezal, the hapless woman from central Washington who became an international spectacle when she pretended to be African American. Or the dust storm created when eighty-year-old Calvin Trillin published a poem asking "Have they run out of provinces yet?" about changing fads in American Chinese food. Or the St. Paul dentist who shot a beloved lion at a Zimbabwe game refuge. This is not to suggest that racial injustice and animal cruelty are not causes for anger and condemnation. They are. But the digital age—with its building waves of self-righteousness—allows the entire world's moral judgment to land on a single flawed individual.

It is almost impossible to talk about outrage—particularly public, media-driven outrage—without also thinking about shaming and bullying. As Jon Ronson put it in his TED talk, "A day without a shaming began to feel like a day spent picking fingernails and treading water." Ronson pointed out that our culture, particularly our online culture, prioritizes ideology over people. I don't think we can separate people from their ideas and thoughts and worldviews, but people are messy. And they make mistakes, and they hurt others. And they do dumb stuff. Myself included. My kids included. My mom and dad and sister. My husband. My co-workers. And I don't think our human weaknesses and failures can hold up to the outrage of an all-knowing, morally superior planet. I don't think some poor college professor who said something stupid or a city council member who cheated on his wife or a sad-sack nineteen-year-old who made an idiotic joke on Twitter can withstand the hopped-up outrage of the world's masses, either.

Plus, outrage is cheap. Social media creates a perfect platform for us to present our fury without having to take much additional action. It's fun, it's affirming, and our expression of shock and disgust can be started and finished before our extra-hot latte is up on the bar. There is also a bit of peer pressure behind it. If I don't weigh in on the latest horror, will my friends forget that I really do oppose police brutality? Will I seem as if I am complicit in the face of injustice and cruelty?

It becomes routine. Pick up dog food: check. Schedule daughter's orthodontist appointment: check. Express my dismay and righteous anger at the drone strike that killed fourteen children at a wedding: Check check check. As journalist Michael Miner put it, the current version of public outrage is something "less like genuine fury than like prissy indignation."

I really don't want my friends to think I'm callous toward injustice, and sometimes I do feel so powerless and overwhelmed in the face of suffering and cruelty that a little burst of "this just really pisses me off" releases some pent-up steam. But that said, is it possible that the constant expression of outrage actually flattens out the differences between minor offenses and true injustices? In the dog-eat-dog world of social media and public protestation, somehow the law-enforcement murder of an unarmed child becomes equivalent to the remark the dean made about my outfit in the elevator. It's all crappy, but I fear our breathless expressions of outrage are making us a little morally sloppy. In the same way that Cheetos dull our senses toward the subtler flavors of cauliflower and turmeric, a steady diet of outrage dulls our ability to discern between degrees of harm or—even more worrying—dulls our ability to feel and act on actual outrage when it's called for.

Plus it can't be good for us—physically, emotionally, or spiritually—to be so fired up all the time. It's just straight addictive, which means of course that we need a bigger and bigger hit off the outrage pipe to feel the flush of self-righteous anger course from our scalp to our toes.

As Tim Kreider put it in his essay in the *New York Times*:

> A couple of years ago, while meditating, I learned something kind of embarrassing: anger feels good. Although we may consciously experience it as upsetting, somatically it feels a lot like the first rush of an opiate—a tingling warmth on the insides of your elbows and wrists, in the back of your knees.

In other words, I may be bored or sleepy or sick to death of my boss, but I know that I can rely on somebody—somewhere—to do something so morally repugnant that I can get my heart rate back up and can sit a little taller in my chair.

All this propping up has a cost, though. It seems like half

the people I know are talking about adrenal fatigue—their limbic systems being burned out by too many stress hormones, specifically adrenaline and cortisol. I know adrenal fatigue is in some ways a prestige condition, associated with too much important work and nonstop busyness, but our return visits to the outrage pool can't help.

And it makes us sitting ducks in the face of huge media outlets and political parties and other hucksters and master manipulators who want us to do their bidding either in the marketplace or in the political sphere. I recently learned of a concept in poker—a game I do not play—referred to as "tilt." The idea is that when a player is overcome with emotion, she can't play at the top of her game and starts making errors. As one commentator puts it, "Tilt is the road rage of poker." The common wisdom among poker experts is that once tilt sets in, the player should walk away from the table because she'll be easily led into mistakes. It benefits the other players at the table to draw a hothead into tilt because they can take advantage of her irrationality and lack of control.

That sounds familiar. It seems as if I spend about 75 percent of my political attention wrapped up in some sort of fuming, irrational tilt. While I fuss and rant and carry on and celebrate my superiority, the cooler heads in the penthouse suite at Fox News or gaveling the Democratic Convention can count on me to be in an adrenaline-fueled stupor and in no condition to think critically or hold them accountable. That is no state in which to pull the voting lever or even write a tweet.

But I know that outrage is also a protective shell separating me both from my own moral confusions and misgivings and from others who have become pawns in the game of "I'm good and you're evil." It creates a "one-strike rule" by which we write off people—even people we know—as unreconstructed and unworthy of genuine fellowship if they say something we deem worthy of outrage.

I'm afraid all this excitable rightness blocks our moral and empathetic imaginations, relieving us of the burden of having to imagine ourselves into the circumstances of not only the noble and the victimized but also the oppressive and the wrongheaded and the bumbling. Last winter, the occupation of the Malheur National Wildlife Refuge in eastern Oregon by a group of right-wing antigovernment zealots led to a lot of hand-wringing superiority here in the progressive enclave of 97214. My little community is not full of folks who look sympathetically on the taking over of federal property by armed men or rhetoric about the free rangeland of the West. In my world, those people represented ignorance and racism and gun-fetishization. They seemed to symbolize just what is wrong with America in the early twenty-first century. This was self-congratulatory outrage-bait of the first order.

And then the thing that now seems inevitable happened. Just as the occupation was ending, there was a confrontation between some of the occupiers and the police out on the highway between Burns and John Day. The police shot and killed LaVoy Finicum the day before his fifty-fifth birthday. Finicum had been a visible member of the occupying band from the beginning, making himself available to news media and leading tours of the refuge. So when he was shot and killed, the news media widely reported it, repeating Finicum's quote from early in the occupation: "I'm not going to end up in prison. I'd rather die than be caged. And I've lived a good life."

That next morning after the shooting, an acquaintance of mine—a person I admire—wrote on her Facebook page:

WHAT IS UP WITH LOCAL MEDIA MEMORI-
ALIZING LAVOY FINICUM WITH GRAND SYM-
PATHY? STOP PERPETUATING THE ROMANCE
OF THE WEST. YOU ARE MAKING ME SICK AND
YOU LOOK UNPROFESSIONAL. THIS IS NOT THE
REVENANT. GET A GRIP. DRY YOUR EYES.

(CAPS in original)

The comment was immediately reinforced with over a hundred likes and twenty comments by people saying they were "sickened" by the media coverage and that they couldn't give a fuck whether Finicum was a great Adele fan. There was a lot of speculation about how the media might have talked about LaVoy Finicum if he had been a young black man. There were offers to go on local radio to discuss the disgusting nature of the media coverage.

My stomach sank a little. I mean, I had been full of bile and judgment over the occupation just twenty-four hours before, but Finicum's body wasn't even cold and here we were outraged—outraged!—over the fact that the local news media might tell the story of a man who was shot and killed by law enforcement.

I think it's fine to feel like the coverage was over the top. Maybe it was. And they were probably right that a young African American man shot and killed by the police would never be humanized by the media in the same way that Finicum was. But the callousness with which these people talked about the death of another human was bracing. This was a person whose parents welcomed him into the world like the miracle he was, a person whose knees shook as he started kindergarten, a person who had a wedding day and nervously held his first child. This was a person who loved Adele. This was a person. And yet because his ideology was other than ours, people I know and like were chiding the media to "dry their eyes."

I'm afraid that's where outrage is leading me. Away from apprehending the complex mix of disappointment and anger and sadness and loss and confusion that would cause a person to leave his family for a month, take over federal property, and then provoke a fatal shoot-out with the police. Away from knowing that not only had LaVoy Finicum not made it to his next birthday but that the officers who shot him will have to remember that evening for the rest of their lives and that the others in the car with him are going to see LaVoy Finicum drop to the ground over and over as they dangle on the edge of sleep.

But that's a complex mix of feelings for the cycle of righteous outrage that we have established for ourselves: *Event, outrage, reaction, outrage over the reaction and probably over the outrage. Distraction. Do it again.* It's such a prescribed and protected loop that grief and wonder and confusion don't have a chance to intrude.

As Laurie Penny put it in the *New Statesman*:

Because the truth—the real, unspeakable, awful truth—is that we are all vulnerable, and afraid, and more ignorant than we'd like to be. We are all fumbling to find a place for ourselves in this weird, anxious period of human history, stumbling between the savagery of late capitalism and the rage of the dispossessed.

Here's the thing: We're humans. We're animals. We're mortals. We're kin of honeysuckle and honey badgers and one another. Sometimes every last one of us behaves nobly and sometimes we behave callously and idiotically. As I write this, I am reminded of the New York poems by the Spanish poet Federico García Lorca. Lorca hated New York and was awash in despair and self-doubt when he lived there. The poem that sticks with me is called "New York (Office and Attack)," translated by Robert Bly. It starts here: "Beneath all the statistics / there is a drop of duck's blood." But it really gets going here:

> Every day they kill in New York
> ducks, four million,
> pigs, five million,
> pigeons, two thousand, for the enjoyment of dying men,
> cows, one million,
> lambs, one million,
> roosters, two million
> who turn the sky to small splinters.

There is no looking away with Lorca. He sees right through the layers of the constructed and the civilized to the tender, the fleshly, the suffering. And he is infuriated at those who would ignore it: "I attack all those persons / who know nothing of the other half. . . . / I spit in your face." But his fury is self-implicating, self-immolating, and brimming with offering. He does not sit back and bark for us to "dry our eyes" but rather offers himself in sacrifice to those who suffer:

> I offer myself to be eaten by the packed-up cattle
> when their mooing fills the valley
> where the Hudson is getting drunk on its oil.

That is a form of outrage that is fierce and sacrificial, one that is incompatible with our laptop version that is cool, clever, and smug, devoid of struggle or self-recrimination. That is outrage tempered in love.

April 2017

A GNOSTIC BILL
OF RIGHTS

A Gnostic Bill of Rights

Lucky is the lion that the human will eat, so that the lion becomes human. And foul is the human that the lion will eat, and the lion still will become human.

—The Gospel of Thomas

I.

"*CITIZENS UNITED.*" WHAT? I TILTED MY EAR A LITTLE and turned up the radio, which up to that point had been a kind of murmury soundtrack to my morning commute. I thought the interviewer had asked some doctor from a prestigious clinic about the causes of the recent explosion of opioid abuse in the United States. But the answer seemed out of sync somehow. I was only half listening, not unconcerned but expecting the answers I thought I knew: the one about globalization and the loss of manufacturing jobs, the one about cheap drugs being hustled across the border from Mexico, the one about workplace injuries and pill mills and the downward spiral to street drugs.

Honestly, I'm rarely surprised by what I hear in the news anymore. I mean, I might be surprised by the news itself, but I am rarely surprised by the analysis. I am relentless in my pursuit of input. Walking, running, brushing my teeth, sweeping the kitchen, peeling potatoes, waiting for a child to finish a rehearsal, I use almost every spare second for input. I love it all: newspapers and Twitter and podcasts and magazines and radio interviews and novels and essays and poems. And because of all that input, people like me—and I know there are a lot of us—become experts not necessarily on the content, but on the analytic stance of the news, particularly of the *New York Times* and public radio variety. We are accustomed to the story of a particular person's struggle that then telescopes out to the full national or global scope of the problem, followed by an expert explaining the underlying causes and what he or she is doing about it. While those reports are informative, they are rarely surprising.

But this time I stopped. I pulled the car under a big full-leafed maple near my ex-husband's house and listened to the interview properly. The doctor explained that once corporations were seen as "persons" with the full rights of free speech, they could take their mega-budget marketing machines straight to human people, offering them a vocabulary for symptoms and brand names for relief alongside soft-focused promises of a more vibrant life. As a result, patients are in a position to plead knowledgeably and persuasively with their doctors, beginning the cycle of pain, relief, addiction, cutoff, street dealers, relief, abuse, overdose.

And to complicate matters, because campaign contributions are considered to be political speech, which is the pinnacle of constitutionally protected speech, those same corporations—including some of those that manufacture and sell very lucrative pain medications—are throwing money at congressional campaigns and state legislators and super PACs, giving elected officials every incentive to look the other way as the cycle picks up speed and more and more Americans descend into addiction and—for some—into overdose and death. Consider this: Drug overdoses are now the leading cause of death among Americans under fifty.

Since *Citizens United v. The Federal Election Commission* was decided in January 2010, it has been a favorite target for the activist left, good governance advocates, and late-night television. That case—quoting an earlier decision written by then Chief Justice Rehnquist—drew this farcical-sounding conclusion: "The Court has thus rejected the argument that political speech of corporations or other associations should be treated differently under the First Amendment simply because such associations are not 'natural persons.'"

Justice Stevens—bless his heart—laid out the more humanistic view in his dissent: "Although they make enormous contributions to our society, corporations are not actually members of it." These two sides of the debate led to the famous dustup a week later between President Obama, who called out the decision in his State of the Union address ("With all due deference to separation of powers, last week the Supreme Court reversed a century of law that, I believe, will open the floodgates for special interests, including foreign corporations, to spend without limit in our elections. . . . I don't think American elections should be bankrolled by America's most powerful interests or, worse, by foreign entities"), and Justice Samuel Alito, who broke the stony-faced protocol of the court, shaking his head and mouthing "Not true" in response.

A few years later, corporate personhood went head-to-head with human personhood again, this time in *Burwell v. Hobby Lobby*. In that case, the question was whether the Affordable Care Act violated the Religious Freedom Restoration Act when it required employers to include birth control in all health-care plans. On the last day of the 2014 term, the Supreme Court found that the birth control requirement substantially burdened Hobby Lobby's free exercise of religion. The court concluded that the law was designed to protect persons, that there are persons inside the corporation, so voilà!, the corporation is protected like a person. Another dissent, this time from Justice Ginsburg: "The exercise of religion is characteristic of natural persons, not artificial legal entities."

And now here is a doctor laying one of America's most significant public health crises squarely at the feet of corporate personhood. To be clear, I think some of what bothers me about corporate personhood is just the audacity of the metaphor itself. There is profound hubris in granting "personhood" to legal constructs that often show very little humanity toward those whom the court has taken to calling "natural persons." For a country that purports to be so solicitous of the miracle that is human life, it seems a little heretical to then claim we get to grant personhood to Johnson & Johnson by a one-judge majority.

How about if we just said, "Yes, corporations have essential functions in this society, and there are times when their rights need to be protected, so let's sort out when those times are and what precisely needs to be protected"? Then we can talk about those protections as corporate rights. Why do we have to transform them into actual living, breathing people? Isn't it just cynical and wrong to conclude that Monsanto somehow needs the same solicitude, care, and protection as a child? Or as an elk? Or a protozoa?

But I am mulling other, more concrete and time-sensitive questions, too, like, How do we get ourselves out of this neoliberal globalistic corporate-loving mess? And how do we come closer to a humane society in which we recognize our own frailties and failures or grapple with its baked-in injustices or pull back from global climate catastrophe or even look out for one another in the face of overwhelming power and wealth?

I know I am far from the first person who has struggled with these questions or their antecedants. One of the charming things about Americans is that we always think we are the first ones over the hill. Each successive generation presents itself with renewed vigor and certainty, ready to take on the struggles of the day. It's sweet, really. It's like the way my dog greets me with the same combination of desperation and affection whether I've been on a grueling month-long work trip or I've walked down to the gas station for a Diet Coke. It's new every time.

Yes, we have been here before, more than once. And we will be here again. But there is one time that was particularly significant to the DNA of the nation—the period leading up to the adoption of the Bill of Rights.

To review, a catfight broke out near the end of the 1787 Constitutional Convention over whether or not a specific enumeration of individual rights was necessary. The new states had called a convention because the Articles of Confederation that loosely joined them in a "league of friendship" were not enough to hold the new nation together. Ultimately, those in favor of a cohesive national government—who came to be called the Federalists—won the day, replacing the flaccid Articles with a newly minted Constitution of enumerated national powers. Just as the delegates dared hope they might be able to gavel the convention and go home, Virginian George Mason called for a separate statement proclaiming the specific rights and liberties of individuals. The exhausted delegates rejected the idea in short order, agreeing with the Federalist argument that an enumeration of individual rights was unnecessary because the right to govern at all was derived wholly from the people and that all rights not specifically granted to the government by the Constitution would be retained by the people.

The debate didn't die there, though. Throughout the ratification process in the states and during James Madison's successful campaign for the House of Representatives, the question of a statement of rights and liberties surfaced again and again. Ultimately—for reasons both political and aspirational—Madison began drafting a proposed set of amendments, which he presented to the newly convened Congress in the summer of 1789. The debate was contentious and full of what one member called "ill-humour and rudeness." And yet, after weeks of argument in the midst of a heat wave that killed twenty in New

York alone, Madison prevailed, and Congress agreed to a set of twelve proposed amendments, which were sent to the states for ratification. Ten of those amendments—which we now know as the Bill of Rights—were adopted in December 1791. The two amendments that remained unratified both concern Congress itself—one imposing congressional apportionment (which eventually found its way into federal statute) and the other prohibiting Congress from giving itself a pay raise (which in 1992 was adopted as the Twenty-Seventh Amendment after a 202-year ratification process).

Think about those days in the summer of 1789: Members of Congress came and went. They were crammed into small hotels and boardinghouses. They debated mornings and took lunch and dinner together. The pavement was pocked and pigs still roamed the alleyways. As a vote grew close, the tone was tense but decorous. Throughout, it was stupefyingly hot. Imagine that last day of debate. While Madison much preferred to be behind the scenes, other members surely looked to him for leadership. The sweat formed right where his wig met the nape of his neck. Just damp at first, not enough to draw attention, a mop cloth pressed discreetly to the spot. But then a rivulet. Needle thin, obeying gravity down the channel of the spine, under the collar, picking up speed all the way to his waistband. A fan, a handkerchief, a walk (counterclockwise to stir up the breeze)—all provided relief, but only temporarily, from the burdens of the body.

Today, as our members of Congress consider whether to strip 20 million Americans of their health care or whether to expel 800,000 young people from the country, air-conditioned Suburbans with lead-colored windows pull into underground garages. Their occupants sweep into a room kept at a perfect sixty-eight degrees, winter and summer. Stuffed chairs: soft, but not too soft. A laundry service. A doctor on call. Water (no ice) and coffee (1% milk, two Splendas) appear and are whisked away throughout the day. The body is pacified and pampered into submission and invisibility.

Yet, for the first time, as I write this, I see the connection between *incorporated* and *corporation* and *corpus* and *corporeal*. Even as we strive to push away the rough edges of our own messy embodiment, we play God. We have gifted moneymaking legal fictions with a corpus—incorporated them—and then breathed life into them. And even still, there are limits. There are no bones, no blood. There is no lust or wonder, no existential terror in the middle of the night. Corporations are not laid up by love or childbirth or open-heart surgery. They do not weep before a sunset or a car wreck.

Baboons and house cats and guinea fowl are closer to us in that regard. And yes, it is difficult to have this conversation without the question of fetal personhood rearing its head. And maybe that's as it should be. Let's stop trading sound bites. Let's have it out. It *is* a moral question. It is a hard question. It is a question that sends people to their knees. And it has since the beginning of childbearing. Let's live in the anguish. Because if we don't, Hobby Lobby gets to argue that its moral decision-making is equivalent to mine and yours and that of the trembling teenager sitting in the waiting room of Planned Parenthood.

Let's be honest. We don't have a very trustworthy track record on personhood in this country. We have been morally confused on this topic on more than one occasion, so perhaps a little humility is in order.

But we are offered some guidance by Madison's preamble to his draft of the Bill of Rights—though it was never adopted and ratified—which starts here:

> The government is instituted and ought to be exercised for the benefit of the people, which consists in the enjoyment of life and liberty, with the right of acquiring and using property, and generally pursuing happiness and safety.

There's something in that intention that rights my thinking. As we consider *Citizens United* and *Hobby Lobby* and our dishonorable history, it's not just that extending what are essentially human rights to corporations puts another brick on the scale in an already seriously unbalanced system, but it wrongly suggests that the dilemmas of corporations and the struggles of humans are equivalent. Corporations are created, maintained, and governed for one purpose—to maximize profits. To do otherwise would violate their charters and their fiduciary obligations to their shareholders. So, when we say that corporations are "persons" who exercise free speech and religion just like me and my neighbor and Black Lives Matters activists and the Buddhist monk who immolated himself in protest of the Vietnam War, we are suggesting that they are grappling with the same anguished questions. But they're not. They are created and programmed to know the answer no matter what the question: make more money.

So while we humans muddle through our mixed-up stew of thoughts and terrors and affections, we do it alongside—or really inside of—a system where profit motive is elevated to the level of our most basic questions of right and wrong. And we start to get confused. We start to think making money is the same as exercising our conscience, or at least the same as balancing disputed, imperfect human values.

But Madison isn't buying it. He points out that the Bill of Rights is for people and our small concerns like "the enjoyment of life" (I love that—what a joyless public life we have experienced as of late) and "generally pursuing happiness and safety." So perhaps the Bill of Rights might offer us a human-scaled version of what it means to be an American and what it means to be a human person living in the company of other human persons.

And perhaps it is ours to reclaim or, as some would argue, claim for the first time. I recognize that it is an untrustworthy document from an untrustworthy and brutal era for so many of my friends and neighbors. But I don't want us to toss it away. I want us to make it our own and with it build a more just, trustworthy, and resilient society. The bones are there. It is mine for the taking. It is yours for the taking. The rights are ours. If we are to become the citizens who will pass this Republic on in better shape—or at least not worse shape—we are obligated to put the Bill of Rights in our mouths and devour it, digest it, become it. And to have it become us.

II.

IT IS A PECULIAR THING, CLAIMING THE BILL OF RIGHTS for oneself. In fact, I imagine that there may be other amendments that folks want to include in their personal civic litany. In all, there are thirty-three to choose from. Like the Thirteenth Amendment, which abolished slavery. Or the Nineteenth, which gave women the right to vote. Some people might want to include the Fourteenth, which protects individual rights against encroachment from the government. And I would suppose some folks are looking pretty closely at the Twenty-Fifth, which establishes the order of succession following the death or resignation of a president, and it gives the vice president and the cabinet some—shall we say—flexibility in dealing with a president who is "unable to discharge the powers and duties of his office."

As for me, as for today, I am going to stick to the Bill of Rights. But I can't quite make sense of the amendments in the order offered. So I consider them in my own idiosyncratic order. And by that, I don't mean that I offer them from most favorite to least but somehow in the order that opens one to the next. I mean, some are so much closer to me. Some of them I find downright funny. Some of them I adore like cherished poems. So I don't think I am taking too many liberties by reordering them a little for my own purposes.

Here is my order, here is my claim.

Sixth Amendment
(a calling, shattered)

In all criminal prosecutions, the accused shall enjoy the right to a speedy and public trial, by an impartial jury of the State and district wherein the crime shall have been committed, which district shall have been previously ascertained by law, and to be informed of the nature and cause of the accusation; to be confronted with the witnesses against him; to have compulsory process for obtaining witnesses in his favor, and to have the Assistance of Counsel for his defence.

FOR ME, THE SIXTH AMENDMENT IS THE GATEWAY, OR maybe the portal, to all the others. Without it, I would have had no need for snooping around in the intricacies of the Fourth or reading nineteenth-century case law on the Fifth. The Sixth Amendment, in all of its right-to-counsel glory, was my invitation to the party.

And I will tell you this: there is nothing—and I mean nothing—like standing shoulder to shoulder with a brother or sister as they face the full power of the government. I want to say "citizen." I want to say "their government." As in, I want to say: there is nothing like standing shoulder to shoulder with a fellow citizen as they face the full power of their government. But I can't because we've become a nation of maniacs, debating who is in and who is out. "Citizen"—as I've said before—is a beautiful word if we think of it as how we live together in community. But it has become an ugly word as Immigration and Customs Enforcement (ICE) sweeps through courthouses and schools, with its poisonous spotlight swinging back and forth in search of those we have deemed "out." But no matter, it's brother and sister, then. And that's probably better anyway because in this instance, "citizen" might be a little too abstract, a little too distant. After all, the United States accounts for almost a quarter of the world's prisons. And African Americans are incarcerated at five times the rate of whites. Too many of my neighbors are suffering from the trauma of having a family member torn from them, from the financial ruin and the shame and the loneliness. We need to come a little closer. So brother and sister it is.

But let me back up. I went to law school in a cloud of ambivalence, vaguely thinking I might become a labor lawyer. Though I was not entirely sure what that entailed, I loved unions, and I loved the idea of hanging out in a hard hat, standing in solidarity with a crew of autoworkers as they struggled against Ford Motor Company and its soul-crushing assembly line. But labor law turned out to be a little more technical and dull than I expected. Plus, there seemed to be very few ladies milling about in labor law. So it never really stuck.

But then the closest thing to a calling I will probably ever know sank its teeth into me. I took criminal law in my first year, and one thing led to another. By third year, I was spending half my time representing indigent clients in misdemeanor cases. I couldn't bring myself to send people to prison for a living, so I knew I didn't have a future as a district attorney. But criminal defense offered me the chance to become part mystery novelist, part social justice warrior. It was intoxicating.

And to top it off, the Constitution required my presence. I mean, the prosecutor isn't called for in the Constitution, which mentions the president and Congress and members of the Supreme Court. But beyond that, it's only criminal defense lawyers. So, after extracting myself from an obligation to a private firm that had made a pretty lucrative offer, I landed myself in the Federal Defender's Office. Sure, there were plenty of clients who hated my guts, and I had a particularly close call with a client who made a move to strangle me in a visiting room at the state penitentiary, but even on the worst day, I never, ever forgot that I was Constitution-bound to my clients, even the ones who loathed me or made halfhearted attempts to kill me.

There is more than self-proclaimed nobility to it, though. There is also the high-voltage energy generated by the fact that the stakes are so high. In the years since I left the law, I have rolled my eyes at what passes for office drama. As someone goes on about some frustration with a co-worker or a project budget, I'll think: *What are you getting so worked up about? At least nobody's going to prison.*

Sure, like any job, criminal defense has its dull days. There are days of slogging through appellate court cases, parsing facts, and writing sloppy, unconvincing prose. But there are other days, too. Like the day—in the middle of winter—that my investigator and I tracked down a guy at an abandoned mill site who we thought might be able to exonerate a client in a high-profile murder case. We knew he had been bragging about the killing even though our client had been convicted and sentenced to life years before. But we had a bead on the guy, and the encounter was electrified by the fact that he had a known fetish for weapons, particularly of the sawed-off and military variety.

Then there was the time a woman called and told me she wanted to meet. When we sat down with her, she said she had lied fifteen years earlier when she testified that her father sexually abused her as a child. It turned my feminist-sexual-assault-survivor worldview upside down. It rattled my unshakable belief that women don't lie about these things. But there she was, looking me and that same investigator straight in the eye and saying, "He didn't do it. I was sick of him and was trying to get him in trouble."

And there were countless wrenching conversations in lockup, steeling myself to be as direct as possible with other humans who were terrified and angry and desperate and who were facing decades of their lives in federal prison.

At the heart of the whole enterprise, there is a moment that is right and dear: When the judge enters the chambers, elevated above those who are at the mercy of law, it is the companionship of another human that is most tender. It is not lawyer and client. At that point, there is only you and you. There is only the warmth of elbow to elbow, shoulder to shoulder as you stand, heads slightly tilted, breath shallow, alone but for the heartbeat of another broken and imperfect creature.

But—and I don't even like to admit this to myself—proximity to that full-throttle emotion, whether rage or thrill or anguish is contagious. It made me feel fully alive in ways that I have rarely felt since. My people are not ones for living on the edge. No, they fully enjoy the center, and they police any potential edges with Tasers and police dogs. But once I was a full-grown woman, or at least thought I was, the edges were seductive. I myself didn't want to commit a crime, but it was intoxicating to live in the world where transgressions were the norm.

That electric sense of aliveness had other consequences, too. Like this one: I fell sloppily in love with that investigator. A year older than me, a half foot taller, and a mad British accent. Haughty and adventurous. Married. Crackling with irony and willing to laugh in the midst of it all. My first day of work—the week after my honeymoon—I arrived dressed in my black crepe suit and chunky-heeled pumps. It was the best impersonation of professional I could muster given I was the youngest, greenest lawyer they had ever hired. Someone walked me office to office for how-do-you-dos. I am certain I was introduced to everyone, but despite the fact that many of those people became lifelong friends, now looking back on that day, I remember only him. Leaning back in his chair, feet on the desk. Suffice it to say there was a shared toothbrush, ice-cold hands locked on a dark sidewalk, and a stray curl tucked behind my ear in a gesture so furtive and tender that it seemed singular. There was high-strung, overexcited laughter. And tears and recriminations, too. In short, the usual.

It wasn't good for me. My limbic system was running on overdrive all the time. But it was addictive, that combination of transgression and impossible love and just purpose. I'm not sure why I retell all this now except maybe partially for the titillation of remembering being that young and idealistic and aroused. But I suspect I also tell it to remind us that these are human endeavors, and humans act as humans do under the pressures of it all.

Intensity begets intensity, with all its attendant failures and discoveries. One poet I have always admired in this regard is the Israeli poet Yehuda Amichai. In the midst of a new and ever-contested homeland, Amichai does not turn away from injustice and conflict and brutality, but he has a bawdy sense of sensuality as well. We are heroic and romantic. We are civic and sensual. We are flawed. Like this, from his poem "Jerusalem, 1967," translated by Chana Bloch and Steven Mitchell:

> In this summer of wide-open-eyed hatred
> and blind love, I'm beginning to believe again
> in all the little things that will fill
> the holes left by the shells: soil, a bit of grass,
> perhaps, after the rains, small insects of every kind.

But then there is the crash. At least for me. And before I knew it, I was looking around for the next thing. Though I could gin up a story about professional growth and development, it was mostly just too much for me. I didn't really mind the workload, and I loved piecing the cases together witness by witness, fact by fact. I even adored researching obscure citations and arguing the law. It was fun in the way that a five-hundred-piece jigsaw puzzle is fun. And I eventually fell into a pattern of easy friendship with my investigator. But the suffering at the root of the work began to fester. Despite the downed-power-pole-live-wire excitement of it all, the human suffering was immense. The bottomless cruelty of family lives, the merciless systems, the relentlessness of bad choices and brokenness.

Now, when I let myself look into the well of it all, I still feel tremors of shame. Partially for being faithless and reckless with other people's feelings. But more—much more, actually—for walking away from something I know is essential. I was weak. I couldn't take it. Even though I knew and still know that the criminal system is ground zero of racism and injustice and suffering, I couldn't muster the strength of character to stay in it. I couldn't answer—and stay faithful to—the Constitution's call.

Fourth Amendment

*(for all your pocket slapping, you have come up
with sweet damn all)*

*The right of the people to be secure in their persons,
houses, papers, and effects, against unreasonable searches
and seizures, shall not be violated, and no Warrants
shall issue, but upon probable cause, supported by Oath
or affirmation, and particularly describing the place to
be searched, and the persons or things to be seized.*

LORD, LORD, THE FOURTH AMENDMENT IS WHERE THE
Bill of Rights hits the streets, whether it's a 2:00 a.m. facedown
in the gravel arrest or a genteel "Turn yourself in for fingerprints
and booking." It is rifling through glove boxes and jeans pockets
and hard drives. It is a warrant shoved in front of a half-asleep
judge or an excuse about why a warrant is just not possible at the
moment. Under the law, it is all about the reasonableness of the
thing.

And yet it is not the contours of reasonableness that are rat-
tling around my heart at the moment. There have been times
when I have been obsessed by whether it is proper to stop a

person for a broken taillight or whether the founders would have allowed the search of a cell phone. And those things matter. But right now, a lump rises in my throat when I think about the premise of it all—the "right of the people to be secure in their houses."

One of my most cherished early-winter rituals is my evening walk with our big dog, when dark has settled over the neighborhood but my neighbors are just getting home. I love seeing the lights flip on, the goldy glow over the kitchen tables and the living rooms popping with new brightness.

I can't help but think about Joseph Brodsky's *Nativity Poems*, several of which capture the particular sharp sadness of winter dusks. This one, from 1986:

> With the onset of night, so much light's packed
> into one star-shard.
>
> It's like refugees packed into one boat.
> Mind you don't go blind. You, yourself are on the street.

There is a delicious melancholy at being outside in the dark looking in. The people, at that moment, are secure in their homes, greeting their fellow householders, lighting the world against the dark. It makes me feel cast out and yet so glad at the sight of these families reconvening around their hearths, even the hearths that are digitized and projected. The loneliness that I hoard is in direct proportion to the tenderness I feel for those fragile, breathing creatures burrowing into the spot they've claimed for themselves and their people. It's being outside that makes me sensitive to the borders of the inside. And Brodsky knows that, too:

> an orphan, a social pariah, an outcast
> who, for all your pocket slapping, have come up with sweet
> damn all

In these early days of 360-degree Republican rule, I have found myself horrified over and over. I have read Twitter until late into the night. I have protested and called and kvetched with my friends. But the last time I downright sobbed over the evilness of it all was when I learned that the House had voted to overturn an Obama-era prohibition of shooting wolves and their puppies in their dens. Their dens? The puppies?

I'm a multi-decade vegetarian. I'm no lover of hunting, but I am willing to entertain the idea that people might need or might want or should be able to hunt in a reasonable, sporting way. That they should be able to provide for their families or pass down a cherished tradition. But the cravenness of shooting a mother wolf and her pups in their den just feels beyond the pale. Jesus, they are babies. They are sleeping with their mother. And here's the other thing, the one I can barely bring myself to see: It doesn't take that much imagination to extrapolate from those sleeping puppies to the sleeping children of immigrants burrowed into their bunkbeds when ICE kicks down the door.

First Amendment

(in the moment, grotesquely exotic)

*Congress shall make no law respecting an establishment
of religion, or prohibiting the free exercise thereof; or
abridging the freedom of speech, or of the press; or the
right of the people peaceably to assemble, and to petition
the Government for a redress of grievances.*

I CAN'T GO ALONG TOO FAR WITHOUT STOPPING HERE. IT
is the very first amendment, after all. It looks after the *Washington Post* and churches and synagogues and mosques and our
right to gather with our friends. It has created a safe harbor for
the KKK and the internet and the prayers of Native American
inmates. It has protected our right to yell at members of Congress at town halls, and it shields us from the Baptists taking
over our schools. It is the taproot from which a democratic society grows.

And yet—for all of its breadth and depth—if asked, the vast
majority of Americans would summarize the First Amendment
as "free speech." To the extent that we love to believe in our inherent superiority over other mammals, our ability to formulate

ideas and launch them from our bodies is our go-to evidence. It's odd, really, when you start to break it down. Sort of like when I catch a glance of my dog out of the corner of my eye. She's just sleeping on the bed or eating the crust off one of my daughters' sandwiches, and I'll think, *Oh my God, we're living with an animal.* The familiar becomes completely remarkable—and almost grotesquely exotic—in that moment.

So it is with speech. Just consider the mechanics for a second. The speech therapy company Speech Buddies describes it like this:

> The most basic principle of speech production is that all sounds are produced by moving air. Air moves from the lungs to the mouth via the throat. The vocal folds (or vocal cords) vibrate as needed. . . . And then the articulators (mouth, lips, tongue, cheek, palate, etc.) shape specific sounds.

And with that, we tell secrets and call children to dinner and coax others to love. We create and destroy empires. We plead with God. And writing, with our fingers gripping a pen or pressed across a keyboard, we pour out into the world that which is otherwise inside the body. (As Whitman put it in "Song of Myself": "I have heard what the talkers were talking, the talk of the beginning and the end.")

Those practices—those tiny, quirky bodily practices—are also the basis of the vast majority of our conflicts with one another. We have become so good at it, this speaking and writing, that we wound one another with regularity and provoke one another to all forms of violence. You can see why it would be tempting to ban some of it—speech—as much trouble as it causes. But our decision to protect it all is one of the benchmarks by which we have decided to define ourselves and judge everyone else.

For a long time now, the central metaphor in free speech jurisprudence has been the "marketplace of ideas." Justice Oliver Wendell Holmes first introduced the concept in 1919 in his dissent in a sedition case—*Abrams v. United States*—in which the two defendants were charged with attempting to impede the war effort during World War I. Their offense was circulating leaflets—one in English and one in Yiddish—denouncing the war and advocating for a socialist Russia. In a 7–2 decision, the Supreme Court upheld criminal convictions and twenty-year sentences for Mr. Abrams and his co-defendant. Justice Holmes, however, wrote the dissent, arguing that the leaflets should have been protected speech and introducing the metaphor that would dominate free speech thought for at least a century: "The ultimate good desired is better reached by free trade in ideas. . . . The best test of truth is the power of the thought to get itself accepted in the competition of the market." He went on to say, "The truth can be expected to emerge only when all ideas are free to compete for rational acceptance."

I am not certain where I was when I first heard about the marketplace of ideas. I suppose I must have been in David Cole's first-year con-law class, watching him nervously—and in my mind, adorably—pace the front of the classroom. He would walk to one edge of the carpet, narrow face and big glasses pointed down, looking up only to turn and walk back to the opposite edge. Whether or not I heard of it there, on one of Cole's trips across the rug, I do know, from the very beginning, I loved it. It felt right; it felt human-scaled. The market that immediately lodged itself into my imagination was the square—the souk—in Marrakesh.

In my dithering over whether to attend law school, I took a couple of years off. The first year I spent teaching in Japan. The second, I headed for the Trans-Siberian Railway. An American friend (whom I met on my first day in Japan) and I took a ferry from Sakaiminato to Vladivostok and then the long train trip to Moscow. We spent a good part of the summer and fall straggling around Europe along with all the other twenty-two-year-olds. But we kept hearing stories about Morocco, so in November we bought long dark skirts and day packs and took off from Spain, leaving our big backpacks in the ferry station lockers in Seville. The train trip from Tangier, where the ferry landed, to Marrakesh was a dream state—hour after hour of treeless taupe, peppered with the occasional cluster of bright pink and blue houses, then back to taupe. We had received all sorts of warnings about the risks for women alone in Morocco. But the souk in Marrakesh was everything I ever imagined it could be: rolled carpets and bright spices and even what I most feared—a snake charmer, with a cobra in a pyramid-shaped basket. But it is the oranges I remember the most, each stall stacked higher than the next. (Think of Neruda's ode: "Orange / the world was made in your likeness / and image.")

So when the brilliant and awkward and charming David Cole introduced the marketplace of ideas, that is what came into my head—competition between date sellers and spice shops and orange merchants for what is sweetest, most fragrant, shiniest. I suppose the marketplace that Holmes and Cole imagined was the Greek agora or the Roman forum, where philosophers and politicians debated road placement and taxation alongside wine sellers and gossiping householders. But close enough. And close enough to the sweet ten-stall farmers' market that opens in my neighborhood on Wednesday nights in summer.

Oh that it were so! That the competition was just between whether to buy new potatoes or broccoli for dinner. But those markets do not stand alone. Those human-scaled markets—in Marrakesh and ancient Athens and Southeast Portland—are far from the global markets of Tokyo and Dubai and Wall Street. Those massive, consolidated markets—and all they impose on us—are impersonal and distant and impenetrable.

As I think about the metaphor of the market and what it means for us now, I can't help but be reminded of the middle section of Allen Ginsberg's mighty poem "Howl." In that section, Ginsberg rails against a rapacious, corporatist demon, whom he calls "Moloch":

> What sphinx of cement and aluminum bashed open their
> skulls and ate up their brains and imagination?

He goes on from there:

> Moloch the incomprehensible prison! Moloch the crossbone
> soulless jailhouse and Congress of sorrows! Moloch
> whose buildings are judgment! Moloch the vast stone of
> war! Moloch the stunned governments!

And on:

> Moloch whose love is endless oil and stone! Moloch whose
> soul is electricity and banks! Moloch whose poverty is

the specter of genius! Moloch whose fate is a cloud of
sexless hydrogen! Moloch whose name is the Mind!

And on some more after that, which I will spare you for now.

Ironically, though probably not surprisingly, "Howl" was at
the center of a storied free-speech trial in which poet and pub-
lisher Lawrence Ferlinghetti, owner of City Lights Books, and
the manager of the bookstore, Shigeyoshi Murao, were crimi-
nally charged and tried for distributing obscenity. The trial has
been written about many times and was adapted into a movie in
which that twittery James Franco played a credible Ginsberg.
In the end Ferlinghetti and Murao were acquitted, and "Howl"
took its place alongside James Joyce's *Ulysses* as a victor in the
war against the cramped imagination of the U.S. government.

And yet "Howl" and the case surrounding it still serve as a kind
of warning flare. As much as I love the metaphor of the market in
its most romantic form, it remains fraught and dangerous so long
as the orange sellers are faced off against Moloch. This is where we
start to bump up against the false equivalencies underlying *Citizens United*. Sure, my friends and I register to vote and protest
and hold house parties to raise money for our favorite candidates.
But we are not going head-to-head with our neighbors or even the
middle-aged ladies in Memphis who support the other side. That
would be the souk version of the marketplace of ideas. Rather, we
are facing off in a marketplace that includes Monsanto and GE
and Hobby Lobby. When the scale of the market is weighted with
that much money and power and influence, we can't credibly believe that the best idea is bound to prevail. And we cannot have
faith that individual voices, whether they are in Memphis or in
Portland, will be heard over the roar of the machine.

Third Amendment

(get off my lawn)

No Soldier shall, in time of peace be quartered in any house, without the consent of the Owner, nor in time of war, but in a manner to be prescribed by law.

SOMETIMES AMENDMENTS ARE SO SWEET AND CLEAR, they can serve as a palate cleanser, as breath between that which is hard and that which is sorrowful. Let me put it this way: If a guy in camo and combat boots shows up at your front door demanding pizza and a pull-out couch, you're free to refuse.

Eighth Amendment
(coddling the delusion)

Excessive bail shall not be required, nor excessive fines
imposed, nor cruel and unusual punishments inflicted.

THEN THERE IS THE EIGHTH AMENDMENT. THE ONE where we have to contend with crime and punishment and how we are going to handle ourselves when our basest instincts are clamoring for vengeance.

Let's start with "unusual." I suppose the prohibition on unusual punishments must be in part to maintain basic parity from one jurisdiction to the next, ensuring that rogue states don't just go out on their own and start imposing bizarre punishments. But there is also the tiniest thread of ethical compunction inside this prohibition, recognizing that somehow it is unjust to humiliate people, even people who have violated the social contract. For some reason, I am reminded that it is a Class A misdemeanor in the state of Oregon to display a person in a trance. It's my favorite misdemeanor, mostly because it is a recognition that it is somehow wrong to parade someone around when they don't have control of their faculties. And that is connected to the idea that even at our most punitive, we must respect at least the core of human dignity.

But really, what a relief it is to see the word "cruel" written out in the Bill of Rights. It is also surprising, given that cruelty seems to be de rigueur—with efforts to separate mothers and children at the border, to cut Meals on Wheels, to raid schools and offices and courthouses for people who don't have the documents that we reify. And think: the Speaker of United States House of Representatives, Paul Ryan, joking that he had been dreaming of kicking people off Medicaid since he was standing around a keg with Rich Lowry. Think: Donald Trump mocking a disabled reporter in front of thousands of screaming supporters. And think again: an internet troll sending a tweet that was designed to—and did—trigger a seizure in *Vanity Fair*'s Kurt Eichenwald, who suffers from epilepsy.

But under the auspices of the Eighth Amendment, the Bill of Rights requires us not to be cruel, not even to people who have been convicted of crimes. The Eighth Amendment has been invoked in cases involving juveniles and in cases where prison medical care was inadequate, but we—or at least I—think of it most with regard to the United States' tortured relationship with the death penalty.

A quick history: The death penalty came to North America with the colonists and continued throughout the early years of the Republic. Since the late 1700s, there has been a movement among members of various faith communities, alongside others, to abolish the death penalty. In 1972, the Supreme Court decided *Furman v. Georgia*, which essentially held that none of the forty death penalty plans in the various states satisfied the Eighth Amendment.

The moratorium—as it turned out to be—lasted only five years, until the execution of Gary Gilmore by the state of Utah in 1977. The death penalty has been contested ground ever since, with twenty-seven states having active death penalty laws, nineteen states with no death penalty, and four states, including Oregon and Washington, with gubernatorial moratoria on executions. There have been reams written on the death penalty, on the ethical implications, on the theological ones, on the impacts on jurors and judges and executioners.

My own real-life relationship to the death penalty was brief. One case. It came about as in a dream. We had been snowed in for more than a week. We could no longer continue without coffee and wine, so we bundled up and set out on foot to the neighborhood grocery. As we left, we ran into a friend from the Federal Defender's Office. We hugged, and he told me that a death penalty team was falling apart. One thing led to another, and I put together a crack team, one with way more experience than I had. I didn't have an office or an assistant or any infrastructure at all, really. But I had a hankering to go back. A pull, an intuition, an itch. And I found the right people to do it with.

But there is no drama to this part of the story, though there were plenty of sleepless nights getting to the right outcome. The client was profoundly mentally ill. He had been alone in his cell talking to himself for the better part of ten years. He never went outside into the tiny yard, never worked out. He just sat and muttered and sometimes banged his head against the wall. We knew the state couldn't execute him—that pesky Eighth Amendment preventing the government from executing those who are not mentally competent—and ultimately lawyers for the state all but admitted that they probably couldn't execute him. So, after a few months and what seems like a few million conversations, we all agreed to a sentence of life without parole and that was the end of it.

Not long after, our governor imposed a moratorium on all executions. Again, that decision was based on circumstances unique to him. Only two people had been executed in Oregon since the death penalty was reestablished in 1984, and both of them were volunteers. In other words, both of them dropped their appeals and asked for an execution date. And both of them were on John Kitzhaber's watch during his first stint as governor. When Kitzhaber, an emergency room physician, returned to office after an eight-year break, he once again was faced with a volunteer. And this time he decided he was not going to participate:

> They were the most agonizing and difficult decisions I have made as Governor and I have revisited and questioned them over and over again during the past 14 years. I do not believe that those executions made us safer; and certainly they did not make us nobler as a society. And I simply cannot participate once again in something I believe to be morally wrong.

So, in many ways, both in my case and in Oregon as a whole, the Eighth did its job. Eventually. And really only sort of. Despite the fact that the moratorium on executions was reaffirmed by our current governor, today there are thirty-five people on death row. They are housed in single cells—with forty-minute exercise periods each day and the occasional visit from a spiritual counselor—while they wait to be executed by their own government. Three death row inmates have been there since 1988. Three were sentenced after the moratorium was already in place. And I would assume there are at least a handful of new death penalty cases ongoing in the state of Oregon today. Millions of dollars have been spent on trying and appealing death penalty cases, not to mention the cost of running the unearthly and peculiar system within a system that is death row. So despite both moral and legal barriers to execution, the system grinds on, dragging almost three dozen people sentenced to die and hundreds of others—victims, families, lawyers, juries, judges—along with it.

One of the most moving pieces of legal writing I have ever read is the 1994 dissent by Justice Harry Blackmun in the case of *Callins v. Collins*. The court had decided, without opinion, not to review the case of Bruce Callins, an inmate awaiting execution in Texas, a state that has executed more than thirteen hundred people over the past two hundred years. Justice Blackmun, who had both dissented from the moratorium in 1972 and voted to reinstate the death penalty in 1976, began his dissent here:

> On February 23, 1994, at approximately 1:00 a.m., Bruce Edwin Callins will be executed by the State of Texas. Intravenous tubes attached to his arms will carry the instrument of death, a toxic fluid designed specifically for the purpose of killing human beings. The witnesses, standing a few feet away, will behold Callins, no longer a defendant, an appellant, or a petitioner, but a man, strapped to a gurney, and seconds away from extinction.

He marched meticulously through the death penalty jurisprudence of the previous twenty years, pointing out time and again where arbitrariness or bias had succeeded over rationality. In the case's most famous lines, he announced:

> From this day forward, I no longer shall tinker with the machinery of death. For more than 20 years I have endeavored—indeed, I have struggled—along with a majority of this Court, to develop procedural and substantive rules that would lend more than the mere appearance of fairness to the death penalty endeavor. Rather than continue to coddle the Court's delusion that the desired level of fairness has been achieved and the need for regulation eviscerated, I feel morally and intellectually obligated simply to concede that the death penalty experiment has failed. It is virtually self-evident to me now that no combination of procedural rules or substantive regulations ever can save the death penalty from its inherent constitutional deficiencies.

I always thought I would have that first sentence tattooed across my back: "From this day forward, I no longer shall tinker with the machinery of death." And anti–death penalty advocates have widely quoted the fierce conclusion that "the death penalty experiment has failed." There is such moral and legal clarity in these words. But now it is this sentence I find the most humbling and the most true:

> It seems that the decision whether a human being should live or die is so inherently subjective—rife with all of life's understandings, experiences, prejudices, and passions—that it inevitably defies the rationality and consistency required by the Constitution.

I offer this—and the whole of the death penalty mess—as a window into the ongoing struggle between who we think we are and who we actually are. Our aspirations are to be evenhanded, merciful, and equitable even to those who violate the most basic of our social norms. But in practice, we are capricious, vindictive, and vengeful—depriving tens of millions of people of health insurance, turning away from the hungry, and letting people languish for decades knowing that their government has decided they should die. In the end, Justice Blackmun was right. After a career of struggling with rationales and standards of review and a variety of checks and balances, he concluded that we humans have a cruel streak that is fundamentally untamable and that there are some things we just can't be trusted with. Like whether another human being should live or die.

Seventh Amendment
(enough already)

*In Suits at common law, where the value in controversy
shall exceed twenty dollars, the right of trial by jury shall
be preserved, and no fact tried by a jury, shall be otherwise re-examined in any Court of the United States,
than according to the rules of the common law.*

FROM THE GUT-WRENCHING TO THE PRAGMATIC. SEE:
Madison & Co. did throw corporations a bone. They—and everybody else—have a right to a jury trial if the lawsuit is worth
more than $20. That's pretty good, and we didn't have to call
them people in the process.

Second Amendment

(do your ears hang low?)

A well regulated Militia, being necessary to the security of a free State, the right of the people to keep and bear Arms, shall not be infringed.

THESE DAYS, IT SEEMS AS IF THE ONLY AMENDMENT anybody talks about with any regularity is the Second. For the previous eight years and then into the 2016 presidential campaign, there was a steady drumbeat of fear that somebody—I guess the president or the possible future president—was hot to "take our guns." During the fall of 2016, a gun rights website called Bearing Arms claimed:

> What Clinton actually wants to ban are the most common firearms sold in the United States. This includes common hunting rifles, target rifles, many popular handguns, standard rifle and pistol magazines, and if Clinton follows Massachusetts Attorney General Maura Healey's deranged lead, it would result in the majority of firearms designed in the past 100 years being banned.

Meanwhile, after the shooting at Umpqua Community College here in Oregon, President Obama urged us to become "single-issue voters." As he put it:

> You have to make sure that anybody who you are voting for is on the right side of this issue. And if they're not, even if they're great on other stuff, for a couple of election cycles you've got to vote against them, and let them know precisely why you're voting against them.

I have to be transparent: I'm with President Obama on this one. And truth be told, if somebody took a run at repealing the Second Amendment, I'd stand with them. In my mind, guns and ammo just do not rise to the same level of seriousness as free speech and religion. But I suspect I am in the tiniest minority, and I'm not ready to go to the mat over it. This country has a deep fear of tyranny baked in, and right now I know several progressive friends who are actively talking about acquiring guns or at least learning how to shoot them in case the Trump administration either gets us into World War III or requires us to foment revolution. One friend just told me she's considering buying a gun to protect her water stash in case the "big one"—the 9.0 earthquake we've been talking about here in Cascadia for the past few years—finally strikes. I just can't get myself there.

But that said, I must admit that I have a soft spot for the actual language of the Second Amendment. I love the quaintness, the bodiliness of "bearing arms." The concreteness of slinging a strap across the back, the hard rifle stock against the shoulder bone, rubbing a shiny spot on a polyester jacket where it rests.

It's incarnate. It reminds me of the song my daughters used to sing in the car:

> Do your ears hang low?
> Do they wobble to and fro?
> Can you tie 'em in a knot?
> Can you tie 'em in a bow?
> Can you throw 'em o'er your shoulder
> Like a continental soldier?
> Do your ears hang low?

And of course, this is a right that is particularly ripe for puns. Think of it: bear. There is the naked form of "bare," with all its revelatory punch. And then the multiple mammalian forms: grizzly bear, brown bear, polar, koala. Plus it's golden when paired with "arms." There were the memes of First Lady Michelle Obama in her smart sleeveless dresses with the cutesy caption "The Right to Bare Arms." And of course the jokes following Education Secretary Betsy DeVos's assertion that public school staff might need to have weapons on campuses because of the risk of grizzly bears.

But there is also the deeply tender use of the word "bear," as in to endure.

When you think of it that way, it reflects the risk and responsibility of taking on an object that can wound or kill another living being. I suspect that many—if not most—American families bear (to borrow the word) their own stories related to guns. It would be perverse not to start with the generational and ongoing terror of African American families when hundreds—if not thousands—of African American citizens have been shot and killed by police officers who have sworn to protect them. Then there are the police officers themselves who live in fear of guns coming out in a routine encounter on the street or next to the highway. And they have. And they do. And there are soldiers who sign up to protect us, many of whom die in the process and many more of whom come back shattered by the burden of it all.

My family has its own experience with guns that would seem symbolic—or at least metaphoric—if it hadn't been a real tragedy that happened to real people. Here's the lede: My grandfather shot my grandmother's arm off.

This is not a story I know well. Recently I had to press to even find out the year. The location. The barest of details.

This is what I know: They were in central Oregon, hunting. It was 1953 or 1954. The kids—all four of them—were at home or somewhere else. My dad was in fifth or sixth grade. I know it must have been dusty. It must have been fall, deer season, or maybe elk, but probably deer. Someone handed someone a hunting rifle through an open truck window. My grandfather ended up with it. The safety was off. It fired, striking my grandmother's right arm above the elbow. She lost her arm.

I never knew my grandmother to have a right arm, though it was not a topic of conversation. It was just a fact. She wore long-sleeved blouses that covered the stump just below the shoulder, and it wasn't that noticeable, really. Not to me at least. My grandmother did not have a right arm. We knew it was a hunting accident. The stories we did hear were about her pluck and determination after the shooting: Your grandmother—wait, let me give her name, Hazel—Hazel started teaching herself to write with her left hand while she was still in the hospital. Hazel insisted on finishing a blouse that she had started sewing before she went on the hunting trip. Hazel worked at the fabric store well into her sixties and somehow managed to carry those big bolts of fabric with only one arm.

No one talked about what actually happened. Somewhere along the line, I heard that she had been in a hunting accident and that my grandfather—Fred—had shot her arm off. That was all.

When it occurred to me recently that I knew very little about the accident, I asked a few questions. A very few. I got even fewer answers. My dad didn't talk to me about it at all. My mom responded to my tiny questions curtly: "It was a very difficult time for everyone." But it was central Oregon, where the trees are far apart and the ground is bare and dusty. She would have been thirty-two or thirty-three years old. My grandfather, then, would have been fifty-two or fifty-three. They had four kids together. She had one more. He had four more. A gun passed through a truck window from somebody to somebody else. My grandfather was holding the gun when it fired. My grandmother lost her arm.

The only other thing my mother told me: "Grandpa always cried whenever anyone asked about the accident." That was it. And that is one family's burden. Hazel's for sure, who lost her arm as part of her right to bear arms. But Fred, too, for the rest of his life bore the burden of the right to bear arms. And my father, also Fred. And his siblings, Lee and Patty and Lawrence. And their children. And ours.

Ninth and Tenth Amendments
(whatever's left in the woodpile)

The enumeration in the Constitution, of certain rights, shall not be construed to deny or disparage others retained by the people.

The powers not delegated to the United States by the Constitution, nor prohibited by it to the States, are reserved to the States respectively, or to the people.

I KNOW IT IS CHEATING TO COMBINE THE NINTH AND the Tenth, but they are conjoined twins. One of the traits I adore most about Madison is his catastrophic imagination. In the same way that I vividly imagine every life-threatening event that could befall my loved ones, Madison was trying to use the Bill of Rights to plug every potential hole into which authoritarianism could seep.

Every time one of my daughters launches into a new venture—big or small—I barrage her with precautions rooted in specifically imagined tragedies: Wear a life jacket. Cross at the crosswalk. Remember, weed is a gateway drug. Don't place your emotional well-being in the hands of a fifteen-year-old boy. Put your phone on your nightstand when you fall asleep just in case the radiation might give you brain cancer. But to wrap it up, I almost always end the litany with the catchall: Make good choices.

The drafters of the Bill of Rights had some close-up experience with tyranny, so most of the amendments anticipate specific forms of tyranny—unjust imprisonment, capricious arrests, harassment of the press, religious persecution. Including the Ninth and Tenth Amendments, however, was their attempt to hedge their bets. The Ninth establishes that just because some rights are specifically named in the Constitution doesn't mean that no other rights exist. And the Tenth is quite direct—if the powers aren't specifically delegated to the federal government, we keep them.

By the time of the 1789 Congress, Madison was convinced that the biggest threat to liberty in the fledgling United States was an overreaching majority. He was concerned that because power ultimately lay with the people, minority interests would always be at a disadvantage. In his imagination, a bill of rights was necessary to shift not only laws and formal structures but the hearts and minds of the American people—particularly the majority—so that they would not undertake unjust "acts to which they might otherwise be inclined." In other words, he left us a note: Make good choices.

Fifth Amendment

(there's ransom in a voice)

No person shall be held to answer for a capital, or otherwise infamous crime, unless on a presentment or indictment of a Grand Jury, except in cases arising in the land or naval forces, or in the Militia, when in actual service in time of War or public danger; nor shall any person be subject for the same offence to be twice put in jeopardy of life or limb; nor shall be compelled in any criminal case to be a witness against himself, nor be deprived of life, liberty, or property, without due process of law; nor shall private property be taken for public use, without just compensation.

I LEAVE THE FIFTH FOR LAST BECAUSE IT IS MY FAVORITE. There's a lot going on here—grand jury, double jeopardy, due process, all good. But the part I hold close to my heart is known— thanks to *Miranda v. Arizona* and television cop shows—as the right to remain silent. In the text, it is about halfway down—no person "shall be compelled in any criminal case to be a witness against himself."

Take this as the proclamation of an introvert, but there is deep dignity in knowing that we get to decide what we reveal. That we do not have to share the contents of our minds. That we are constitutionally entitled to stay silent. It's not the right to explode, but the right to implode. The right to stand still. The right not to participate. The right to do nothing. We're a country that is so protective of our own exteriority that it is easy to forget that self-containment is both a virtue and a right. But the Fifth Amendment doesn't forget, and neither do the poets.

It appears that nearly every poet writing in English—and probably each of those writing in every other language as well—has written a poem wrestling with silence. Emily Dickinson wrote several, but here is the most famous:

> Silence is all we dread.
> There's Ransom in a Voice—
> But Silence is Infinity.
> Himself have not a face.

Four lines anchored in the weight of silence and yet a recognition that silence *is* the mystery. And there's this one, by contemporary poet Robin Ekiss, that—though it is tremendously less existential than Dickinson's—recognizes the relative preciousness of silence (or even mere quiet) in contemporary life. "The Death of Silence" starts here:

> A car's backfire
> rifles the ear

with skeleton clatter,
the crowd's *walla walla*

draws near, caterwaul
evaporating in thin air.

And she ends here, in desperation:

I'm buried to the hilt
like the knife,

after it's thrown,
continues to bow

to the apple
it's split.

Ekiss recognizes the cost of constant exposure to the backfire and clatter and caterwauling. "I'm buried to the hilt" pretty much expresses how I feel most of the time. My most well-known statement of fed-up-ness, especially when my daughters were young, was "Mama needs to hear her own thoughts."

I am not alone in this. A few years ago, Chloe Schama wrote an article for the *New Republic* called "Silence Is Now a Luxury Product." There she argued:

From noise-canceling headphones to the popularity of silent retreats, there has never been quite so great a premium placed on silence. And not only do we value it in a general sense, we're willing to pay for it. Silence has become the ultimate luxury.

But we cannot—and should not—be lured into treating silence as a commodity, to be doled out as money and circumstance allow. Silence, as Madison and his compatriots recognized, has political implications. Let us not forget that Václav Havel's archetypal example of living in truth—the greengrocer who removes the "Workers of the World Unite!" placard from his window because he isn't really committed to the cause—is actually an assertion of silence. It's not so different from the Jehovah's Witness couple who did not want to display New Hampshire's "Live Free or Die" motto on their license plate. They were fined and sentenced to jail, but, in *Wooley v. Maynard*, the Supreme Court found in favor of the couple, concluding "the right of individuals to hold a point of view different from the majority and to refuse to foster . . . an idea they find morally objectionable." Though the basis of the decision was the First—not the Fifth—Amendment, the impulses were the same: the right to stand silently apart from assertions not our own. Those are the needs of a free society. Those are the needs of a religious minority. Those are the needs of an introverted poet and a reticent founder. Those are the needs of a soul.

July 2017

BECOMING
CITIZEN

Becoming Citizen

I GET A LITTLE SQUIRMY WHEN FACED WITH THE JAUNTY
get-to-know-you question "What is your first memory?" Sometimes I'll fib and mention the birth of my sister or the death of
my grandfather. But I don't really remember those things. What
I do remember is being told about them so many times that I can
picture three-year-old me peeking into my mother's arms as she
presents my pink-flannel-swaddled sister or feel the shock and
grief of my grandfather's sudden stroke and death, but I don't
have any genuine memory of either of those things.

The true answer: Watergate.

Though my sister had been born and my grandfather had
died a few years earlier, Watergate is the first thing I recall.
Not the break-in or the trials or the congressional hearings or

even the resignation of the president, though memories of those things came later and certainly poisoned my and my generation's relationship with the presidency in specific and with government in general.

But my memory, the memory that lives deep in my body, is the sound of the word. Watergate. It sounded dramatic and powerful and slightly scary. Maybe like a dam. Maybe something like the Hoover Dam, though I had not seen the Hoover Dam at that point, not even in pictures. But when I heard "Watergate," I felt a kind of building pressure, like a flood held back. Something towering and concrete and somehow both protective and ominous. All this hinted at by the tone of voice used over the radio—a mix of excited and stern and breathless that I had never heard before.

I was used to not knowing what things meant. But Watergate. I turned it over and over in my mind and then on my tongue, feeling a jolt of electricity down my spine as I mouthed it to myself.

One day, I couldn't stand it anymore. I was in the front seat of our car. My mother was driving. If I do the math, it would have been in the fall of my first-grade year, probably on our way home from school. I know we were just past the curve at the Kingsford briquette plant. The radio was on—Watergate and more Watergate. My skin felt prickly and aroused. "Mom," I finally burst out, "what is Watergate?"

This was a strange question coming from me, given that I was a fundamentally incurious child. At least in that way. Adults didn't talk to children about money or scientific discoveries or political scandals. They talked to children about chores and whether their teacher was nice and field-trip forms. Besides,

I have a dispositional tendency toward secrets. In fact, I love secrets, cherish them like shiny stones in my jacket pocket. I am loath to break the spell of a secret unless the curiosity is so strong that it swamps the gears of my otherwise brittle self-control.

As a child—in those dark days before Google—if I had questions, I rat-holed them away and tried to find out the answer without asking an adult directly, sneaking up on the answer by eavesdropping or by looking things up in the encyclopedia in the hall. But at some point, the word became too huge for me not to blurt it out.

"What is Watergate?"

"A hotel."

"A hotel?"

"Yes, a hotel in Washington, D.C. The Republicans broke into it."

My skin went flat, my mind casting around for what that could even mean. I am pretty sure I had never stayed at a hotel, at least a proper hotel with a lobby and an elevator. I might have stayed at one of those beach motels where cars blow exhaust into your room as they back up into the parking lot. But never one in a big city like Washington, D.C. What did a hotel, as abstract as it was, have to do with the goose-bumpy glamour of a word like "Watergate"? But it was too late. The veil was pierced. And though I later read Woodward and Bernstein and developed a bit of a weakness for the cloak-and-dagger world that was the Nixon White House, it was just gossipy and entertaining and demoralizing. Never again did it feel shimmery and mysterious.

There are other words that hold power over me, like "sacrament" and "St. Petersburg" and "honeycomb." Words that capture my imagination like "uncanny" and "Tukwila" and "pound cake." When I hear them or read them, my body says: Pay attention, write them down, turn them over in your mouth. Most often, now, when I shudder like that, I know the word should go in a poem or in the notes for a poem or at least should be written longhand in my notebook.

Some of the words persist. I get the jitters every time I hear them, even though I have heard them dozens—sometimes hundreds—of times. "Citizen" is one of those words. A persistent one. A long-term one. Along with its companion words—"civic," "city," "civitas," "civilization." "Uncivilized" is one of the great put-downs of our family. Though I prefer the Greeks and their less militaristic ways, I know that the word "citizen" and its cousins are derived from Latin and the Roman sense of citizenship.

Of course, in many instances, the word "citizen" is problematic. It is used as a sword to divide between who is in and who is out, who is "legal" and who is "illegal." So as we talk about how we might live better together in community, we resort to bloodless words like "resident" and "voter." Sometimes we're crass and use the word "taxpayer," and other times we're downright cynical, merging democracy and capitalism and use words like "customer" or "user."

When I say the word "citizen" aloud, I usually ask if we can put questions of legal status aside and use "citizenship" to mean how we live together. How we act in public as we strive to create community. I am attracted to Eric Liu's definition of "citizenship": "a deeper, ethical sense of being a member of the body." And though that definition is much better, even it has a utilitarian tinge. It has little to do with my private, heart-thumping reaction to the word.

My inner version of "citizen" is more existential, I think. There is a sense of aspiration around it, for sure. It's both a little retro and a little sentimental, like red-white-and-blue bunting on the town pergola or a stadium building to crescendo as it nears "the land of the free" in the national anthem. But it also has a kind of weightiness in it that I cannot resist: "I am exercising my rights as a citizen." Or "I am speaking here not as a senator but as a citizen." It is both authoritative and central to one's innermost identity. In that, it seems like something to strive toward, something that I—in my anxiety and self-doubt—have not quite achieved.

I must start by asking: Citizen of what? The word, with all its trembling power, implies a relationship to place, a sense of belonging. And questions of belonging, or not, carry their own wounds. As we rush from the places where we were born— where our ancestors are buried—our sense of belonging has become frayed and sometimes outright shredded. And as millions of people are forced from their homes by war and climate catastrophe, more and more of the world's citizens are far from the places where they feel they belong.

As for me, my belonging sphere is relatively simple, comparatively speaking. Sure, I am a citizen of the United States. And Multnomah County and the city of Portland. But more than anywhere else, I probably think of myself as a citizen of Springfield, Oregon, though I have lived away for more than thirty years and never had an address inside the city limits even when I did properly live there. But I know each curve of the river and what the bracken looks like in spring and then again in fall. I still know the last names of some kids in each graduating class. And I can recall the families who owned the gas station and the feed store. I can still close my eyes and remember what it was like to dodge log trucks as I ran on the gravel shoulder of the two-lane highway in the steady, cold rain. But even that sturdy belonging is relatively recent, a generation or two. All four of my grandparents are buried there, but no one much further back than that.

Potawatomi botanist and writer Robin Wall Kimmerer gets close to the essentials of place-based citizenship: "If citizenship is a matter of shared beliefs, then I believe in the democracy of species. If citizenship means an oath of loyalty to a leader, then I choose the leader of the trees." If I look at it that way, I am also a citizen of low clouds and moss, of straight-backed Doug fir and sword fern. I am a citizen of rain.

But even if we can establish the where and the who, what—and here is the heart of my question—is citizenship calling us to be?

As for me, I am dispositionally unsuited for public life and yet deeply attracted to it. One of the jokes I used to tell on myself was "I went to law school to stop crying. Mostly it worked." What I meant by that is that I was so raw in those days after college, almost anything real led to tears: a heartfelt conversation or a sweet moment on the street between a dog and its person or a soaring speech or a gritty poem. It was exhilarating to live like that, with every emotion so close to the surface, but it was also exhausting both for me and for people I saw more than once in a while. Looking back now, I know I was a little out of control—causing scenes at dinner parties, falling into a weeping puddle at coffee shops. But I was not numb. To basically anything.

Law school turned out to be a good place to get ahold of myself. Daily weeping spells were not an option, and relatively quickly I became acculturated to the linearity that is law school.

I did my best to accept the model and become a rationalist, and it was a pleasant way to live, I must say. The expectations were really clear, the work was really hard, and the competition was all-consuming. Input and output were closely related—hard work to good grades. And good grades were about all that mattered. What a relief that was. I sipped bitter iced coffee all day, created color-coded outlines, compared notes with my friends, and read until my eyes burned. I had a little poetry habit on the side. But I thought of that as a puff of air to keep the inner flame alive while I went about reconstructing an outer self that was competent, clear-thinking, and under control. And, mostly, my very expensive plan worked.

But only mostly. Once in a while, the construct sprung a leak. After leaving law school and D.C. to return home to Oregon, I spent the first two years in the relative emotional safety of a state supreme court clerkship. But when I finished there, I moved to the high-stakes world of the Federal Public Defender's Office. My very first sentencing involved an unarmed bank robbery. The facts, as they say, were terrible. The bank robbery was clear, and so was the identity of the robber—my client, let's call him Mr. L. But Mr. L.—oh poor old Mr. L.—never had a chance. He grew up in an authoritarian, alcohol-fueled, and chaotic family in Minnesota. He was the family scapegoat, and his punishments were both cruel and symbolic—things like locking him out of the house on frozen nights and leaving him behind while everyone else went to eat dinner. He dropped out before he reached high school and wandered from job to job, trailing a variety of illegal substances behind him. By the time we walked into our sentencing, he was in his late forties and nursing a nasty heroin addiction.

I was a bundle of nerves before the hearing, though I had submitted reams of paper on Mr. L.'s behalf. I was dressed in my best Nordstrom Rack suit and a pair of chunky black pumps. Just before the judge was scheduled to take the bench, the prosecutor strolled over to me and mistakenly said, "Hi, Wendy." I burst into tears and said, "Don't do this." His face froze. His eyes jerked away from me and toward the floor. This was clearly outside of federal court decorum. I continued to ugly-cry and wipe my nose with the back of my hand. Then he said: "Jeez, Wendy, it's not personal." "It is to Mr. L.," I snarled back and marched off to the bathroom, leaving him staring at the ground. I came back to counsel table about the same time the judge entered the courtroom, and I did the whole sentencing with tears rolling down my face.

Mr. L. got a hefty sentence—though not as hefty as the prosecutor had hoped for. I can't remember now the exact number, but I do remember the feeling "That is a long time." And besides, I had utterly humiliated myself by acting like a high-strung eighth-grader. I was sure—and probably justifiably so—that I had cemented my reputation in the federal courthouse as an unstable and unpredictable headcase. I spent the next nine years working that off. I never melted down quite like that again, mostly because I undertook a serious regimen of rest, hydration, and breathing each time I needed to go before the court in a charged setting. But every time the phone rang and the court clerk said "The jury's back," I burst into anxious tears.

A few years ago, I was invited to read from my first book at the sweet, private liberal arts university that I had graduated from twenty-some-odd years earlier. It was a bluebird day, and I was full of nostalgia for the warm spring afternoons when I would sit out in the grassy quad with my friends and half study and half doze. The students I met with that day were close readers and eager to talk. The culmination of the event was a community reading. There were several people I knew from my days as an undergraduate—administrators, the chaplain, old classmates. Among them was a retired political science professor who had been my academic adviser and whom I adored. She was a tiny woman who wore jewel-toned saris every day and had been educated at Delhi University, then at Harvard. Her husband had been an Australian botanist, many years her senior, but funny and brilliant and doting. Their international marriage, their academic pedigrees, their willingness to invite students warmly into their lives made them the most cosmopolitan couple a sheltered girl from a timber town had ever even imagined, let alone met.

But there my dear professor was, twenty-five years later, sitting right in the middle of the room, grinning madly at me as I read to a friendly and largely familiar audience. After I finished, I came down and hugged her, thanked her so much for coming, and sat down across from her. I asked about mutual friends and other retired faculty members. She asked about the book and about my classmates and my kids. I was awash in a deep sense of belonging. I felt like a hometown girl done good. And then, after a solid exchange of gossip, she said, referring to two other faculty members we had both known and I had worshipped: "You know H. and D. and some of those other guys, they thought you were fragile. But *I* knew you weren't. *I* knew you were strong."

I felt like she had slapped me across the face. I had not one inkling that those brilliant men—whom I had believed included me in the smart-alecky jokes and political banter—thought I was fragile, that they worried I wasn't strong enough. It took me right back there to those days. Yes, I was always wavering on the edge, between the political and the artistic, between the Enlightenment and the Romantics, between counting electoral votes and memorizing sonnets. I was a student of the enormously externalized world of American politics, but I was hungry to be a *citizen* of the interior world, where connections are gossamer and the mind softens toward the numinous. It's not really what I wanted to be. It's just what I was. And I had no idea that those male professors, whom I also respected and adored, attributed my romantic temperment and multiple loyalties to weakness and fragility.

The conversation that night after the reading could have sent me into a tailspin. Because those four years were defining. For the first time, I followed my own interests. I ate foods I'd never heard of. I took Japanese. I read poems and novels in translation. I made friendships that have survived fights and illnesses and divorces. And I took to heart the university's motto: *Non Nobi Solum Nati Sumus.* Not unto Ourselves Alone Are We Born. In a single offhand remark—even one that had admiration at its core—I felt cast out of that sense of belonging.

But one of the blessings of being nearly fifty years old is the ability and inclination to say "Fuck 'em." Maybe I am fragile and weak. Maybe I am. But maybe that straightforward, strong, sometimes even cynical version of citizenship that those guys—and many other guys—were cultivating isn't getting us anywhere anyway. Maybe I should stop trying to be so tough, stop trying to conform to the crisp professionalism the public realm idealizes.

I want a form of citizenship that makes room for the mercurial, the mythic, the mysterious. I want a form of citizenship that makes room for bursting into tears. Among my most treasured poems is one that Seamus Heaney wrote in celebration of the anniversary of the founding of Amnesty International, "From the Republic of Conscience":

> At their inauguration, public leaders
> must swear to uphold unwritten law and weep
> to atone for their presumption to hold office—
> and to affirm their faith that all life sprang
> from salt in tears which the sky-god wept
> after he dreamt his solitude was endless.

Yes, that's it! We should all be so humble and intimate with the gods. We should all atone for our presumptions.

As I write this, the world is reeling following some brutal months. It's not just the election and realizing that we are not the liberal, pluralistic democracy we touted ourselves to be, though that is bad enough. Last week, the president announced that the United States plans to pull out of the Paris Climate Accord, one of the last best hopes to curb the use of fossil fuels and slow the pace of global devastation. In this country this year, 421 people have been shot and killed by the police, and the year isn't even half over. ISIS-inspired terrorists plowed over partiers on the London Bridge, and right here in my own town, a white nationalist terrorized two teenage girls—one of them African American and the other wearing a hijab—and then stabbed three men, two of them to death, as they came to the girls' aid.

Everyone I know is wringing their hands, agonizing over

the relentless cruelty of it all and fearing for the future. The public sphere, the civic sphere, and the world all seem dangerous and irrational and violent. It is as if the shadow that Jung warned us about and that we have ignored and disowned and denied has burst forth in a terrifying shower of sparks.

I am tired, and I don't feel particularly up to citizenship these days. It feels too chaotic and noisy and contentious. It feels coarse and angry and relentless. In a way that I never have before, I fundamentally sympathize with people who say some version of "I just don't follow politics. It's too depressing." Or "They're all crooked anyway." Or "What can I do about it?"

It used to be that as soon as a president was sworn in, I started looking for news about who was going to show up in Iowa for the Jefferson-Jackson Day dinner. But I just can't muster any glee this time around, even in the midst of the so-called resistance. I find myself feeling like Frodo in the first book of The Lord of the Rings trilogy when he says to Gandalf: "I wish it need not have happened in my time."

I find myself wondering if political life is a young woman's game, and if I am more effective—not to mention less anxious—when I just focus on loving my family, working hard at my job, and perfecting my piecrust. And Lord knows there is plenty to do in tending to my family and my piecrust. And a lot more of that is in my control. But there is a niggling voice in the back of my head whispering *Cop out*, and I know I would be abandoning something essential. I cannot abdicate citizenship to the shouters and the power hungry. None of us can.

But what if we forged a version of citizenship along the

lines of W. G. Sebald and Václav Havel? A version inspired by Mother Teresa and Desmond Tutu? As Havel said in his stubborn loyalty to the individual moral life, "The salvation of this human world lies nowhere else than in the human heart, in the human power to reflect on the human meekness, and in human responsibility." And this from Sebald's devastating novel of the Holocaust, *Austerlitz*: "We take almost all the decisive steps in our lives as a result of slight inner adjustments of which we are barely conscious."

What inner adjustment is being asked of us now? What if we decided to bring more of our full selves to the public square? What if becoming citizen—in this time and place—is a coming out for the inner life, for tender possibilities as well as our doubts and fears and wildest imaginings? As Gandalf responded to Frodo, "So do I . . . and so do all who live to see such times. But that is not for them to decide. All we have to decide is what to do with the time that is given us."

Yes, there will always be Watergate and all the "gates" to follow. And we will need the sharp pencils of Woodward and Bernstein and now their progeny, Maggie Haberman and David Farenthold. And bless their hearts. But what if we were also to allow ourselves to really feel the grief of species extinction and the obliterating loss of those parents whose children die at the hands of terrorists and cops? What if our vulnerability and our tears were essential to our full citizenship? What if we were to bring the joys of walking the dog in the park and meeting a stranger in line at the supermarket to our public life? What if our leaders were to, in the words of Seamus Heaney, "weep to atone for their presumption to hold office"? What if, as the poet David Whyte put it, we were to become "full citizen[s] of vulnerability, loss, and disappearance"? What if we were to admit we are all mortal, flawed creatures, and that we require one another to sort it out? Maybe that is where the word "citizen" reveals its magic and metaphor. Maybe that is where citizenship thrums and shimmers.

June 2017

Buying Our Way Home

I'M TRYING TO MAKE SENSE OF THE QUESTION "WHERE are you from?" It's my favorite of the get-to-know-yous. It seems rude to go straight for the "What do you do?" as if sizing up net worth or number of degrees. "Where are you from?" seems gentler, offering the answerer a range of options—a neighborhood, a town, a continent. Still, it has its own complications. It's often weaponized against immigrants and people of color, suggesting a one-upsmanship of belonging. And in a state that's growing as fast as Oregon, it also gives off a whiff of old-timer chauvinism.

Yet there is something essential about declaring a place as one's own and offering others the chance to do the same. And while I don't want to suggest that anyone belongs anywhere other than where they are right now, I also don't want to fall into the big mass of placelessness that Wendell Berry warned us against in his essential 1969 essay "A Native Hill," in which he wrote of road builders in eighteenth-century Kentucky: "Because they belonged to no place, it was almost inevitable that they should behave violently toward the places they came to."

I tried it out on my daughters: "If someone from another country asked you where you were from, what would you say?" They responded more or less in unison, "Portland, Oregon." For them, it's not even a question to ponder. When I am asked, I usually say, "I live in Portland, but I'm from Springfield, Oregon—from Lane County." When my husband, David, is asked, he answers, "Houston," though he was born in Tulsa, has lived in a dozen states, and has bounced around the same two zip codes in Southeast Portland for more than fifteen years. Luke, my stepson—who was born in Maryland, forged his first memories in California, and spent all of his formative years in Oregon—is firmly on Team Portland.

"What about Springfield?" I asked. My older daughter ended it: "That's where you're from. We're from here."

Though I wasn't surprised, it is existentially unsettling to have my daughters—whom I am closer to than any other human beings—be from a place that I still don't entirely claim as my own. And though there are only 109 miles between unincorporated Lane County, where I grew up, and inner Southeast Portland, where I live now, that 109 miles makes a difference—topographically, economically, culturally. So they are from Portland, I am from Springfield, and David is from Texas. But what does it mean when each member of a family living under one roof answers that question—"Where are you from?"—so differently?

This is the story of America, and, in particular, it is the story of the West. I can't help but think about Thomas Jefferson and how he set us on the path for all this rootlessness. Jefferson, sitting on his porch in central Virginia, imagined Americans into the "fertill and handsome valley" that Lewis and Clark found at the end of their expedition. Of course, that fertile valley was already well inhabited by the Kalapuya and the Clackamas, the Chinook and the Molalla. But Jefferson, with all his idealized musings and irreconcilable frailties, sent a pack of white Americans off to his "Garden of the West" to strengthen the perfect agrarian Republic, based on a noble relationship to the land and a commitment to small-scale self-governance.

As many people before me have written, it is impossible not to wonder how the drafter of one of the world's great paeans to liberty and self-determination could be responsible for both perpetuating slavery and setting in motion the displacement of thousands of indigenous people. I also wonder how a man who had never been west of the Blue Ridge could have had such a deep imagination and voracious appetite for the lands on the other side.

But here we are—a mishmash of descendants of this place's original residents and transplants pulled west by the first Homestead Act and the Dust Bowl and then another desperate Homestead Act and then the World War II shipyards and then, most recently, by gushing food critics writing for the *New York Times*. And people keep coming, looking for something, and adding more fancy townhouses and traffic in the process. On darker days, I wonder if the very basis of the Republic as Jefferson conceived it—his notion that self-governance depends on small communities intimately connected by place—has been worn out by contemporary life, by tremendous cultural forces spinning us away from, rather than toward, a mature and orienting sense of place.

I wonder if we are not the road builders whom Berry called "placeless people." As he described them: "Having left Europe far behind, they had not yet in any meaningful sense arrived in America, not yet having *devoted* themselves to any part of it in a way that would produce the intricate knowledge of it necessary to live in it without destroying it."

Even I—whose grandparents met on Main Street in Springfield and whose mother was born in Lane County and whose children were born just a few miles from the house they live in now—question my bona fides. Am I really *from* here? Like many Americans, I yo-yo between the restless desire for the imagined better place and the yearning for a burrowed-in sense of belonging. I have ancestors from Virginia and North Carolina, Connecticut and Arkansas, England, Denmark, and Germany. They are displaced Cherokees and Bavarian Catholics and cranky combatants who fought for the rebels in the Civil War. And those are only the ones I know about. Though I am almost always the old-timer in the room when the question of when did you get here—"here" meaning Oregon—comes up, even I am a newcomer to this place, relatively speaking, and I am a first-generation resident in the ecosystem of my neighborhood. All that makes me question my own perceptions, my ability to interpret the smell of the air just before dawn, the day the first leaf turns, the migration of songbirds and geese.

The first poem I published as an adult was written soon after my second daughter was born, when I was struggling to orient my children in and to this place. It was called, tellingly, "Native

Species" and drew on familiar—and maybe tired—images of this place: osprey and great blue heron, huckleberries and hazelnuts and salmon.

Looking back now, I see that poem as reflecting a persistent need to claim my children for this place; in fact, the setting of the poem was the McKenzie River in east Lane County, so even then I was trying to claim them for *my* place rather than the one they would ultimately call their own. But it is also part of a whole body of "western" literature and visual art that adopts surface motifs for a place: some of them beautiful and moving and authentic, and some of them—like mine, I fear—serving as a received shorthand for genuine place.

IF I WERE LIVING IN THE LANDS OF MY LONG-AGO ANcestors, would there be a cellular, or at least inherited, recognition of other markers of place, ones I cannot imagine past the flashy heron and the overworked salmon? Although all of these images have their roots in this place, they also represent a kind of anxious iconography, a way both to claim the children and reclaim the landscape in a predictable, inherited, and tactile way.

It has become part of cocktail-party wisdom to blame the spread of Bed Bath & Beyond and Home Depot and Walmart for the loss of local culture, community spaces, and even regional dialects. But is it possible that the opposite is also true? Could it be that as we grasp for familiar domestic markers—received and corporatized as they are—we warmly invite Bed Bath & Beyond into our communities as a kind of cultural hot-water bottle? Do we need a designed and focus-group-tested lexicon of home because we no longer live among our ancestors' bones, because we do not know the high-water mark of the river, because we are not intimates with the creatures among us? Is it possible that in our wanderings and resulting isolation we actually need—or at least crave—recognizable and mass-produced images of home?

We have looked to Bed Bath & Beyond and the others to create a sense of place, and they—whoever they are—are more than willing to oblige; in fact, they have created a compelling image of home that they count on us to identify with and purchase whole. And though the particular anxieties are different, we are, like Tolstoy's Ivan Ilych, buying a version of home that reassures us of not only where we are but also who we are:

> In reality it was just what is usually seen in the houses of people of moderate means who want to appear rich, and therefore succeed only in resembling others like themselves: there are damasks, dark wood, plants, rugs, and dull and polished bronzes—all the things people of a certain class have in order to resemble other people of that class.

Is it possible that we are grasping for symbols of home and place because we are maimed in our ability to live genuinely where we are? Is the Jeffersonian dream of shared governance based in place dead beyond revival? Do we need to just concede to the Federalists, surrender to the competing forces of the market, and continue nattering on about local salmon and huckleberry jam?

I hope not. But I think it will take both as-yet-unpracticed alertness and tremendous humility to try to re-create a relationship to place, to wherever we find ourselves now. We'll have to swim upstream. We'll have to admit that we don't know exactly what our place is, that it doesn't belong to us anyway, and that it will require our finely tuned attention to keep us from falling victim to easy icons. And we may have to use tremendous creativity to notice or make our own, more genuine sense of home.

What I am grappling with here is the distinction between the *idea* of living in place and the *fact* of living in it. The question I am asking is not how to conceptualize living here—in my little square of 97214—but how to *actually live* here. That's the question my daughters were answering, and that's the one I often overlook. I like the idea of place, so I am particularly vulnerable to images that feel settled or cozy or tucked in. I understand what it is to want to feel at home in place and to resort to buying proxies for place, substitutions for genuine close observation and stewardship of home.

I know there is humility and unsettledness inherent in the admission that this place does not belong to me. It did not belong to my ancestors in the past, it likely will not belong to my descendants in the future, but I belong to it now, and I have the chance to pay attention, to be present here, now. That admission of transitoriness, of mortality and ephemerality, is humbling and frightening, but it also connects me in a new way both to this place and to unexpected ancestors and descendants. It connects me to the Chinook people who most certainly cultivated, or at least knew, the ground that is now my fussed-over little garden. It connects me not just to my own imagined grandchildren but also to the imagined grandchildren of the woman who lives in St. Louis and the one who lives in Oaxaca who will occupy this place next. And it connects me to the grandmothers of Tulsa and Reykjavik who are tending the plot of land that my granddaughters may live on someday.

It nudges me to ask, What gratitude do I owe the generations that preceded me even though they are not my biological ancestors, and what stewardship do I owe those who follow, unrelated though they may be in the traditional sense of the word?

So in that sense, Jefferson was right—not in the way he envisioned virtuous white farmers anchoring a place-based Republic, but maybe in an even deeper way. If we can bring ourselves to attend to the place we inhabit now—even if we cannot say "I am from here"—we can at least say "I *am* here," and treat that hereness with particular humility and alertness to cues we might not otherwise recognize. We can embed ourselves in an intergenerational web of care for place and for those who pass through it. We can be part of a community that both precedes and follows us, creating an intimacy with past and future that grounds us here, now, making mortality a little less lonely and bringing our children a little closer, even if they are from a town 109 miles away.

March 2012

The Rim of the Wound

An Open Letter to the Students of Columbia University's Multicultural Affairs Advisory Board, with a Special Note to My Own Daughters

---

DEAR ONES, I READ WITH INTEREST YOUR RECENT OP-ED in the *Columbia Spectator* arguing, among other things, that Ovid's *Metamorphoses* should be assigned with a trigger warning because of the story "The Rape of Proserpina." As you put it:

> *Metamorphoses* is a fixture of Lit Hum, but like so many texts in the Western canon, it contains triggering and offensive material that marginalizes student identities in the classroom. These texts, wrought with histories and narratives of exclusion and oppression, can be difficult to read and discuss as a survivor, a person of color, or a student from a low-income background.

Clearly you struck a nerve, because there's been a lot written about your letter and what it means for higher education. As I'm sure you know by now, some people are supportive and sympathetic to the hurts and horrors that might lead a young person to need a trigger warning in the first place, while others cluck-cluck over how thin-skinned and coddled kids are these days. They fret that your parents—and all contemporary parents, which I guess includes me—are so protective and over-involved that students are unable to withstand even the slightest discomfort or challenge to their ideas.

That latter line of argument makes me a little defensive, being both a mother of daughters and a sexual assault survivor myself. I'm concerned about young women like you and my daughters—when they are old enough to get there—being safe at college. It ought to be beyond argument that students who are combat veterans or sexual assault survivors or victims of other traumas should be able to immerse themselves in the world of ideas without unnecessarily reopening old wounds. And I am tired of the mom being blamed for every one of society's perceived weaknesses.

I'm your friend. I'm a feminist. I'm old enough to be your mother. I want what you want—a world where injustice is chased into the night by fierce kindness and right action. And yet it made my heart sink a little to watch four bright, passionate young women toss *Metamorphoses* onto the bonfire and prepare to light the match. Yes, the Western canon is too white, too male. I made the same argument when I was an undergraduate thirty years ago. And unfortunately, it's still true.

But let's stick with the specifics of "The Rape of Proserpina" for a moment. Many of our readers will know it in its Greek form, the story of Demeter and Persephone, though the version I love is the translation by poet Ted Hughes, and he retains the Roman version. As a refresher, here are the highlights: Ceres, goddess of the harvest, was busy making the Roman Empire a fertile and productive place until the giant Typhon—who was buried under Sicily—started "vomit[ing] ashes, / Flame, lava, sulphur." Pluto, god of the underworld, feared his roof would collapse, so he came to the surface to check for damage. Aphrodite saw her opportunity to bring the chaos and mischief of love to the nether regions, so she goaded Cupid into shooting his arrow deep into Pluto's heart. Proserpina, Ceres's daughter, was gathering flowers in a field with her friends, and "in the sweep of a single glance," Pluto became mad with love. Being the god of the underworld, he kidnapped a terrified Proserpina and took her to his kingdom as his wife, which sent Ceres into a fit of rage and grief. She ransacked the world and demanded Proserpina's return:

> Then she slew man and beast in the furrow
> With an instant epidemic, throughout the island.
> She broke up the ploughs with her bare hands,
> Forbade the fields to bear a crop
> Of any kind. She made all seed sterile.
> This island, that had boasted its plenty
>
> Throughout the world, lay barren.
> As soon as the blade showed green—the grain died.
> Floods, heatwaves, and tempests
> Sluiced away or dried and blew off the tilth.
> The bared seeds were collected by birds.

Ceres's negotiating position was seriously strengthened by her relentlessness, so Jupiter—the mightiest of the gods and Pluto's brother—arranged for Proserpina to return to the world of the living. But unfortunately for Ceres, Proserpina had violated one of the conditions of the underworld by eating seven seeds of a pomegranate. As a result, she was allowed to come back to the surface for only half the year. For the other half— one month for each seed she had eaten—she returned to Pluto and the underworld, dividing both her time and her nature between dark and light, between cold and warmth, between sunny meadows and the depths of hell.

It's a stark tale. Proserpina is kidnapped, raped, and held hostage by the king of the underworld, and that is nasty, violent business. Though I had probably heard the story sometime before I arrived at university, I didn't study it seriously until I read *Metamorphoses* as a freshman. That was the same year I was sexually assaulted by a classmate. And that was a nasty, life-changing business as well. One I didn't want to be reminded of in honors literature. And one I don't want to be reminded of now. And one I don't want to write about in an essay that you and my children and parents and co-workers might read. But I do write about it because I know that I am one of the 20 percent of American women who will be sexually assaulted in their lifetimes. And I write about it because my identity—including my identity as a survivor—has changed over those years, and so has my relationship to the myths of *Metamorphoses*.

In the nearly thirty years since, I've turned to the tale of "The Rape of Proserpina" and its Greek counterpart again and again despite the horrible bluntness of title and the violence at the center of it. The story—like all great metaphors—keeps opening up. As a young woman, I found sisterhood in the brutalization of Proserpina. It wasn't just the rape that was familiar, but the sudden descent into darkness despite all my efforts to stay in the light. It was also the confusion of connecting to a deep, sometimes frightening, inner life while being expected to be smiling and presentable in the outside world. Later, it was the tug-of-war between being a daughter and being a wife.

In recent years—for obvious reasons—it's been Ceres I look to for comfort. Of course, I worry myself sick about my own daughters' safety and whether some dark lord will pluck them out of my motherly nimbus. But Ceres is so much more than a doting mother. Despite her devotion to sunny wheat fields and the fruits and flowers of the world, Ceres has a fierceness that is not to be trifled with. One of my favorite moments in the story is when she takes a break from her desperate search for Proserpina to drink from a jug of water infused with barley and herbs. A "cocky brat" jeers and calls her a "greedy guzzling old witch." But he does not know who it is he's mocking. Ceres throws the jug of broth in his face, then slowly and methodically shrinks him, transforming him into a newt. Believe me, as an adult, educated, professional woman who sometimes finds herself the impatient recipient of what has brilliantly become known as "mansplaining," I wish I had a jug of barley broth and the power to transform someone into a reptile. But at least I can turn my inner eye toward Ceres and know that she has—and through her, I have—the last laugh.

Truth be told, I even recognize the impulses of Aphrodite. Though I hate to admit it even to myself, it has sometimes been sorely tempting to use the "tickling barbs" of love (or at least desire) to move the needles of power, to—as Aphrodite put it—"expand our empire."

Shit happens, ladies. And it's unfair. And I hate it. And I wish it weren't that way. But I want you to have the full range of tools to keep becoming the badass women you are meant to be. Can you imagine what it must have been like two thousand years ago with no heat, no air-conditioning, no emergency broadcasting system? "The Rape of Proserpina," along with many of the stories in *Metamorphoses*, offered a human-scale rendition of that which is fearsome and capricious and unexplainable—earthquakes, violence, winter. And for all the intervening years, the stories have offered companionship as we struggle with great mysteries and great pain, including the pain of being raped. But we are not bound to take myth literally, and we are tough enough to use it for our own purposes. As the American poet Louise Glück puts it in "Persephone the Wanderer":

> You are allowed to like
> no one, you know. The characters
> are not people.
> They are aspects of a dilemma or conflict.
>
> Three parts: just as the soul is divided,
> ego, superego, id. Likewise
>
> the three levels of the known world,
> a kind of diagram that separates
> heaven from earth from hell.

This is not to suggest that you and your friends are the biggest threat to metaphor in the culture. But I do want you—along with my own daughters—to be the ones with access to the mystery. Now I fear that the most well-known metaphors are those being offered by advertisers. Of course, capitalism—the market, as we quaintly call it—has no incentive to generate myths and stories that sit with us in our grief and confusion and anger. It has every incentive to use metaphors and symbols to try to convince us that with enough money and consumer goods, we can buy anything, including everlasting beauty and immortality itself. Tales of suffering and disaster are not particularly useful in selling moisturizer.

But let's be real. Immortality is not for sale. The thing that is making us feel unsafe is not a collection of ancient myths; it is the fact that the world is *not* safe. I don't say this to excuse violence or racism or colonialism or oppression. But I do say it to wake us up. The world will never be safe enough to save us from our own deaths. Or even our own suffering. By turning away from myths that grapple with pain and violence, we are turning away from the companionship of the immortals.

And in my book, the immortals go far beyond my favorite dead white guys—Ovid and Dante and Blake. When I am casting about for guides—or at least traveling companions—in the perilous swamps of the inner life, I turn not just to them but also to the dreamlike novels of Gabriel García Márquez and Isabel Allende. I lie awake poring over the numinous images of Adrienne Rich and Vénus Khoury-Ghata. I seek out the stories and poems that touch the unconscious, that hang around when confusion and despair threaten to overtake me entirely.

I am in search of art that is rich in what the Spanish poet Federico García Lorca called *duende*. The word *duende* itself refers to a foul little goblin that appears in Spanish myths and fairy tales, but in Lorca's construct, *duende* is the sense of earthy foreboding that brings the artist face-to-face with death. It is *duende* that gives flamenco its devastating combination of vitality and desperation. As Lorca put it, *duende* is "a sort of corkscrew that can get art into the sensibility of an audience . . . the very dearest thing that life can offer the intellectual."

I hate to be the one to tell you this, but from my advanced age, it is looming loss and death that increasingly injects intensity into the hours of my life. There are days when I cry all the way to work, knowing that our days are numbered, knowing that I will drop these particular children at these particular schools only a few more times, even if the repetition sometimes seems enough to make me chew my foot off. I am keenly aware of the dangers of the world, the ones facing my daughters and the ones facing you. But the awareness of impermanence makes it (almost) impossible to take even the carpool for granted. So I'm with Lorca when he stands on the edge and cries out: "Pain is made flesh, takes human form, and acquires a sharp profile. She is a dark woman wanting to catch birds in nets of wind."

I don't write this to bust your chops for calling out Ovid, but it is a dangerous thing for a culture to lose access to the language of the unconscious. As my grandmother might have said, you are bright as a shiny penny. But I will add this: You—like all of us—are bound to confront the darkness sooner than any of us would like. And if we turn our faces away and pretend that winter will never come, we are doomed to live under fluorescent lights in climate-controlled family rooms, taking selfies and preserving only that which is singular to us. Then what? We will have chosen our own imprisonment, a conscription to a world of surface, corporatized images, fearful of that which reminds us that we are bound for pain and death. And if we are unable to look into the face of suffering—our own and that of others—we seal ourselves into our own individual experiences that we replay in their particularities, cut loose from the arc of human experience.

It is a frightening thing, reliving trauma, but our souls—as Lorca put it—"love the rim of the wound," and myth lays down a path for us to find each other across cultures and millennia. Come close, dear ones, let's walk the path together. I'll reach for your hand. I hope you'll grab mine back.

August 2015

Where the World I Know and the World I Fear Threaten to Meet

ON APRIL 21, 2014, KATHERINE LOUISE POWELL DIED OF breast cancer. She was not quite forty-seven years old. Kitty and I met when we were barely out of adolescence. Two rural Oregon girls, recent college graduates, trying to sort out our places in the world. Soon after, she headed off to Stanford Business School while I started at Georgetown Law. We saw each other now and then, but a few years later, we came home, found jobs, got married, had kids. Once we got through the grind of breastfeeding and diaper bags and shoe tying, we made a commitment to see each other at least once a week. Every Friday morning, before sunrise, we laced up our shoes and walked and talked—about our kids and our husbands, about our ambitions (both the noble ones and the self-serving ones), about alternatives to incarceration and policies to slow climate change, about the vagaries of the health-care industry, about whether market solutions had any place in solving civic problems, and in the end, about her illness and most certain death. And then one Friday she was too weak to walk, and there were weeks of running back and forth to her house. And then she was gone. Just like that. Forty-six years old. Four kids. A brilliant career in health-care reform. She was just gone.

It took me almost a year to take our weekly walks off my calendar. And now, I am left with the hollowness of her absence, of course. And filled with love and worry for her family. But it is also an experience like no other to witness the illness and death of a bright and vivacious person at the peak of her life. Terminal cancer exposes us to the body—suddenly organs that have been invisible and flawless send us into waves of wracking pain. As the plump layers of vitality fall away, the skeleton reveals itself in ways that we never see in our healthy and distracted lives. Walking, eating, breathing—all of it becomes both miraculous and laborious.

Since then, several more young and seemingly healthy friends have been diagnosed with cancer. My father had deep brain stimulation surgery to curb the increasing symptoms of Parkinson's. Some of the symptoms got better. Some of them got worse. And if that were not enough, I turned fifty this past summer. I feel it. And not just in my knees or when I catch a glimpse of the crepey skin across my throat that looks just like my grandmother's, but I feel it in my bones somehow. And even deeper than that, I feel that I am going to die. And so will everyone and everything I love.

In the midst of this swelling sense of morality, I began to

hear the expression "white fragility" emerging in the cultural conversation. Whenever I'd hear it, I'd find myself bristling and think: *Damn straight I'm fragile. And so are you.*

The scholar Robin DiAngelo coined the term over a decade ago, but it started picking up steam recently to describe the deep discomfort that many—maybe even most—white people display when forced into a conversation about race and racism. There are anguished and outraged articles and hilarious and pointed videos all recounting times when white people crumpled in the face of a frank discussion of race, diverting attention and sympathy back to themselves and making it nearly impossible to unpeel and honestly address layers of racial oppression and white supremacy.

DiAngelo defines "white fragility" to be "the state in which even a minimum amount of racial stress becomes intolerable, triggering a range of defensive moves. These moves include outward display of emotions such as anger, fear and guilt, and behaviors such as argumentation, silence and leaving the stress-inducing situation." DiAngelo, who is white, describes something real and pernicious and dangerous. The basic idea is that white Americans are often so unpracticed in considering race and racism—which is in and of itself a massive privilege granted by whiteness—that they collapse into a moral and emotional crisis when confronted with evidence of persistent and systematic racism.

I know I have indulged in the grasping, guilty, insipid weakness that DiAngelo warns against. Too often I am thin-skinned and conflict-averse and afraid to look too closely at the overlapping oppressions of this culture and how I might benefit from them. I am afraid to look at how the very idea of whiteness is at the center of a system of cruelty and suffering. That is an ethical failing that I—and many other white people—need to own up to and try to correct.

But all that said, I still bristle at using "fragility" as a corrective or, worse, as an insult. It suggests that we should toughen up and take what the world has to offer. That we should outgrow our petulant fragility.

This is where I part ways with DiAngelo.

I want us to claim fragility. I want us to own it. I want us to face up to our fragility rather than shun it—or worse—hide it from one another. Maybe I can offer DiAngelo a replacement term: "white weakness" or "white insecurity" or even "white preciousness." But I want to save "fragility" to mean something more bodily and more existential. In fact, I am developing a hunch that by turning toward the deep knowing that we are actually fragile—flesh and bone and mortal—we become less like the shallow and trembling people DiAngelo describes.

This hunch springs partially from my own experiences and the vagaries of aging and loss, but it is also informed by the writing of Ta-Nehisi Coates, who incisively picks apart the central fallacy behind white supremacy, which is not just the world's most persistent strain of racialized oppression but is also a construct contrary to the human condition, the condition of living in a body. In his book *Between the World and Me*—an extended letter to his teenage son—Coates pierces the bubble of what he calls "the dream," a version of whiteness that is tidy and protected by capitalism and baked-in white supremacy. And he is provocative in his conclusion:

I am convinced that the Dreamers, at least the Dreamers of today, would rather live white than live free. In the Dream they are Buck Rogers, Prince Aragorn, an entire race of Skywalkers. To awaken them is to reveal that they are an empire of humans and, like all empires of humans, are built on the destruction of the body. It is to stain their nobility, to make them vulnerable, fallible, breakable humans.

It is hard to read Coates's words without becoming either defensive or passive in the face of them. It is tempting to either pull out a litany of my own suffering or accept his worldview wholesale in a sort of guilt-addled stupor. But his thinking is too serious for either path.

What Coates is calling us—particularly white people—to do is to wake up and confront that which is dark and brutal and, yes, fragile. But here's the news you already know. Ours is a culture—and here I mean white majority culture, such that it is—that walks into the house and throws on every light. We will do almost anything to hide from the dark. We spend heaps of money and precious years trying to insulate ourselves from death and suffering by trying to pretend that we are exceptional, that we are exempt from the human condition. In our refusal to look directly at human frailty and death, we chase after that which is impossible, leaving a trail of rapacious consumption and injustice in our wake.

And if we can't face up to our own vulnerability and ultimate mortality, we sure can't do it on behalf of the planet, which is as fragile in our hands as it has ever been.

The last hours I spent with Kitty alone, she was in and out of sleep. She had been confined to bed for days at that point, but her loved ones were stopping in to sit with her. By then, she had coalesced into what was essential—bones and skin, breath and tiny sips of water. That day, that last day I was alone with her, she asked me to read to her. I had *Song of Myself* on my iPad, so I just started from the beginning:

> I celebrate myself, and sing myself,
> And what I assume, you shall assume,
> For every atom belonging to me as good belongs to you.

She closed her eyes and kept them closed.

> There was never any more inception than there is now,
> Nor any more youth or age than there is now,
> And will never be any more perfection than there is now,
> Nor any more heaven or hell than there is now.
> Urge and urge and urge.
> Always the procreant urge of the world.

I kept reading. She kept sleeping, her breathing shallow but steady. I read one section after the next until I reached the beginning of Section 7:

> Has any one supposed it lucky to be born?
> I hasten to inform him or her it is just as lucky to die, and I
>   know it.

> I pass death with the dying and birth with the new wash'd
>   babe,
>   and am not contained between my hat and boots,

And peruse manifold objects, not two alike and every one
   good,
The earth good and the stars good, and their adjuncts all
   good.

"Read it again," she said.

"What?" I responded.

"Read it again," Kitty whispered. "He's so brave." "So brave,"
she repeated and closed her eyes. I read that section again and
then kept reading for a few more minutes, a few more sections.
She didn't say anything else that afternoon, just breathed and
held my hand and listened until I had to slip away to work.

That poem, the one Whitman worked on for his whole life,
as he says, "contains multitudes," a lot of it expansive and brash
and sometimes downright self-promotional. And yet it was in
his quiet confrontation of death and decay that Kitty found solace, that she felt strength and saw courage.

French geophysicist Xavier Le Pichon argues that fragility
is actually what makes the earth a living being. He writes of the
strengths and weaknesses of the tectonic plates and how they
interact to create the dynamism of the earth's surface. And now
he is applying those theories to the earth's sentient inhabitants.
In a recent interview Le Pichon said:

> I think it's going to be a big discovery in life sciences when
> they realize the importance of the fragility of human life and
> the fact that the human life is really so fragile that it needs to
> create a whole new way of culture, of dealing with the others.
> The fragility is the essence of men and women, and it is at the
> heart of humanity.

In another essay, Le Pichon argues that only by confronting fragility and mortality can we imagine life beyond our own limited selves:

> As humans are confronted to suffering and death, as mirrors of their own suffering and death, they are confronted to their own fragility and vulnerability and this confrontation forces them to go beyond themselves by entering into a transcendent world that can be metaphysical, artistic and (or) poetic.

That particular brand of clear-eyed and elegiac thinking calls on us to maintain a kind of dual consciousness, or if we are particularly good at it, multiple consciousnesses. We are called to be attentive to the grocery list and yet aware of the rough crossings of our ancestors. It calls us to be present and connected parents while remembering that our parents did the best they could while holding the suffering of their parents and the parents before them. It is knowing that while I live in a relatively safe neighborhood under a relatively intact roof with relatively clean drinking water, that is not true for everyone, not even everyone I know. It is holding on to the knowledge that there are Iraqi sisters the same age as my girls who have never lived in a world without war. It is knowing that right now, while I boil water for coffee, someone is plotting a brutal attack to wreak suffering on strangers, ablaze with some imagined eternal glory or earthly notoriety. It is staying awake to the fact my now perfectly functional organs could turn on me in a second. That kind of multiple consciousness is the only seed for strength. The only seed for empathy.

It is in our inner lives where that kind of consciousness can

arise, where we may start to break down the fear-driven constructs that keep us unwilling to look injustice and oppression
in the face. In that space, there is hope that we can hold our own
sufferings and failings and frailties and not cling so hard to the
identities that protect us from seeing clearly our role in the suffering of others. By accepting our own fragility, we have nothing
more to grasp at, nothing more to hide from.

Tracy K. Smith, in her poem "Duende," gets close to that
inner state and the clarity that follows:

> If I call it pain, and try to touch it
> With my hands, my own life,
> It lies still and the music thins,
> A pulse felt for through garments.
> If I lean into the desire it starts from—
> If I lean unbuttoned into the blow
> Of loss after loss, love tossed
> Into the ecstatic void—
> It carries me with it farther,
> To chords that stretch and bend
> Like light through colored glass.
> But it races on, toward shadows
> Where the world I know
> And the world I fear
> Threaten to meet.

Oh! I love the line "If I lean unbuttoned into the blow." That
embrace of suffering and loss and fragility bears no relationship
to the weak-kneed ninnyism that Robin DiAngelo describes

and in fact—in Smith's version—it sets us on the path to meet the world that we most fear and that we most need to confront.

As I grapple with loss and aging and what seems like impending fascism and imminent climate catastrophe, it often comes down to questions of what is fragile and what is strong, what is mighty and what is weak. In my confusion and sadness and sometimes outright despair, I often return to that last afternoon with Kitty and her clear-eyed recognition of the strength and courage that come from embracing our own weakness and certain death. Only then, when we strip away all that is inessential, can we look squarely at what we are facing and indeed what we are—flawed and mortal and, yes, fragile. Only then can we get a glimpse of what Xavier Le Pichon calls the "heart of humanity," and only then—hopefully—can we take a breath, stand strong in the face of cruelty, and inch closer toward justice.

December 2016

What Is My Job Anyway?

*Grappling with the Burdens and Blessings
of Emotional Labor*

WE COULD SET OUR CALENDARS BY IT. PRACTICALLY OUR clocks. Every year, on the evening of December 23, my husband and I have a big argument. Usually around 11:00 p.m. He and I can go weeks—sometimes months—without ever exchanging a cross word. But in the eleven holiday seasons we've spent together, we've always had a blowout that same night. The subject is always the same, though sometimes I start it. Sometimes he does. Sometimes there is just a spontaneous conflagration. The problem? Me "overdoing" the holidays. By that time, I am running on fumes, sleep deprived and ragged, and usually unshowered. He is fed up with overscheduling and oversocializing and around-the-clock forced jocularity.

As for me, I start thinking about the holidays right after

Labor Day, and by December 23, I am in the home stretch. I don't want to create the wrong impression. We don't go in for expensive gifts. We're not a family that drops money on electronics or trips to Hawaii. Mostly we try to give what is needed—warm pajamas, a decent sweater that can get each of us through until spring, a wooden spoon to replace the one the dog chewed up. Lip gloss and face cream. Sparkly pens and notecards. The only real extravagance is books. Piles and piles of books.

But there is baking and party-hosting, and there are cards and letters to friends I see only rarely now. I feel acutely the burden of memory-making. I want our kids and their friends and our friends and neighbors and visitors and strangers walking by to feel warm and cared for, to have an indisputable sense of belonging. I know that the work of belonging is daily work, but there is so little ritual in American life anymore. It's as if—in the Catholic sense—all time is ordinary time now. Except the winter holidays. And I feel the weight of their singularity intensely.

Last year, early one morning during the week after Thanksgiving, I took our four-month-old puppy out so he could do his 3:00 a.m. prowl around our postage-stamp backyard. He had to sniff and growl at his reflection in the patio door and backtrack and root around under the hydrangea bush, so I scrolled through Facebook as I shifted from one bare foot to the other on cold concrete. Several friends and acquaintances had posted an article from *Huffington Post* titled "Holiday Magic Is Created by Women. And It Is Killing Us." Mostly it was an article extolling the basics of what we have come to call "self-care"—yoga, decaf green tea, sleep, letting things go. But it was the subtitle that captured my attention: "The emotional labor women do this time of year threatens our mental health."

Over the past year or two, it seems like suddenly everyone is talking about "emotional labor." Some headlines: "4 Ways Men Can Take On More Emotional Labor in Relationships (And Why We Should)"; and "I Said 'No' to Unpaid Emotional Labor by Saying Goodbye to This Word"; and "Women Are Doing Double the 'Emotional Labor' of Men—and Still Aren't Getting Enough Credit."

It turns out that the idea and the expression was coined by Berkeley sociologist Arlie Russell Hochschild in her 1983 book, *The Managed Heart*, to capture a very specific market phenomenon—the commodification of emotion for the comfort and enjoyment of customers. As she put it, "I use the term *emotional labor* to mean the management of feeling to create a publicly observable facial and bodily display; emotional labor is sold for a wage and therefore has *exchange value*."

Much of Hochschild's research focused on the training and working conditions of those women (and a few men) whom we then called "airline stewardesses" and now refer to as flight attendants. To cut to the chase, Hochschild concluded that the central question in flight-attendant school is "How do you rid yourself of anger?"

The culture has, with a vengeance, picked up where Hochschild left off. And as the headlines indicate, we have become champion emotional-labor boundary-setters. We hear it in the rise of "it's-not-my-job-ism": It's not my job to educate you about my experience. It's not my job to make you feel comfortable. It's not my job to plan the office birthday parties. It's not my job to control my emotions for your benefit. In fact, it's not my job to consider your feelings at all. Though we've strayed from Hochschild's original definition, her spirit is most certainly alive in the cultural debate about who does what for whom and whose feelings matter.

Not surprisingly, there is a great deal of overlap in the conversation about emotional labor and the one about domestic labor. It is all part of what the cantankerous twentieth-century priest-critic Ivan Illich called "shadow work"—work that is unseen and essentially unassigned but that greases our social lives and makes the lumps and bumps of human interaction seem a little less hostile and a little more friendly. It is the labor that contributes both to fellow feeling and to society building.

Part of the connection between these realms is that many of us who worry about such things throw ourselves into domestic labor as a form of emotional labor. In other words, we stay up half the night writing Christmas cards or baking cupcakes or scrubbing the kitchen floor because we want to make friends and co-workers and family members feel comfortable and welcome and cared for. I am a cradle-raised feminist for sure, so my commitment to the domestic is not out of some postwar sense of what American life should be like. But I do harbor the increasingly out-of-fashion belief that I actually am at least partially responsible for the experience of the people around me, and I don't want to do them wrong. Despite the years that have passed between the publication of *The Managed Heart* and now, Arlie Hochschild nails it again: "We have a simple word for the product of this shadow labor: 'nice.'" As she says, "There is the moral or spiritual sense of being seriously nice, in which we embrace the needs of another person as more important than our own."

I recognize that this whole snarl of expectation and obligation has a nefarious place in the history of women's struggle for liberation and in the oppression of people of color who are expected to do what they can to keep white people comfortable and safe. Virginia Woolf took on the issue directly in her 1931 speech "Professions for Women," in which she advocates that women writers must kill the "Angel in the House" in order to follow their own interests. Woolf said of the Angel, "She was intensely sympathetic. She was immensely charming. She was utterly unselfish. She excelled in the difficult arts of family life. She sacrificed herself daily." Woolf insists that she could not be both the Angel and the writer who has thoughts of her own, many of them not tender or sympathetic or selfless. Had the Angel of the House lived, Woolf insists, "she would have plucked the heart out of my writing."

Often that's what's at stake when people say "It's not my job to coddle the emotions of everyone around me." They—or rather we—are being clear about what we can and can't do for others in order that we may attend to the tasks and interests that vivify us and that give our lives meaning separate from the happiness and comfort of friends, family members, co-workers, and strangers.

And yet I am still unsettled by the surging, widespread dismissal of emotional labor. The term—as we use it today—goes much further than Hochschild's original, fairly limited definition. Now many of us have embraced the term to set firm boundaries around the shadow work for which we are not compensated or even recognized. By saying we will no longer engage in unpaid emotional labor, we are saying: It is not my job to take care of anyone's emotional life but my own. It's not my job to make sure my husband and kids write thank-you notes. It's not my job to plan retirement parties. It's not my job to soothe co-workers who are struggling. It's not my job to smile at strangers in the grocery store. Or make small talk on the bus. Or offer a kindness to a passerby on the street.

And while I absolutely understand the point, here's a true confession: I want to do all those things. In fact, I want to do more of them. I want to smile at strangers more, offer more surprise gestures of kindness. I want to help defuse anger with listening. I want to make my husband and children feel particularly taken care of because I make their sandwiches just the way they like them. And I want Christmases and birthdays to feel like occasions that sweep them—and all of us—out of ordinary time.

The recent denunciation of the burdens of emotional labor is seething with resentment. And, boy, do I understand resentment. I am, after all, the one who fights with her husband every December about the emotional labor of the holidays. But, I don't want to be relieved of that work. I am resentful, for sure. But most of my resentment is not at having to do the emotional and domestic work but rather at not having it seen, recognized, and—as petty as it sounds—appreciated.

As I struggle through the slop of desire and obligation and resentment, I can't help but wonder if part of the problem isn't framing solicitude and care for others as a "job" in the first place. I wonder if it isn't rooted in the fact—as Hochschild intimated thirty-five years ago—that we have commodified everything, including emotional control, expression, and affect, which has destabilized our ability to value caring work without expecting economic compensation or public recognition.

We have long since become a nation of specialists. We—and by this I mean middle-class we—outsource everything from lawn care to breakfast. Largely invisible others—many of them economically and legally vulnerable—labor on our behalf in factories and restaurants and often in our own homes and yards. We cook from scratch less, rarely repair anything ourselves, and make virtually none of our own clothing. In the workplace, we produce one or two things—at most—and are expected to purchase the rest. The household, which was once a primary unit of production (think cottage industry), has become an insatiable and irreplaceable consumer.

So it's not surprising, really, that we should outsource and corporatize emotions and emotional experiences. According to Hochschild, flight attendants are asked "to see the passenger as a potential friend, or as like one, and to be as understanding as one would be with a good friend." The problem with that framing in a commercial context, however, is that there is no reciprocity. "The passenger," as Hochschild points out, "has no obligation to return empathy or even courtesy."

The more we treat emotional work—the worrying, the cajoling, the smoothing of feathers—as labor to be hired out, the less likely we will see it as what humans do to care for one another and keep society running. As Hochschild pointed out:

> It does not take capitalism to turn feeling into a commodity or to turn our capacity for managing feeling into an instrument. But capitalism has found a use for emotion management, and so it has organized it more efficiently and pushed it further.

As it turns out, there are other, broader consequences of commodified emotional labor. Because we have become conditioned to think that it's someone's job to feel and act in a particular way for our benefit—and because it has become corporatized and commodified—we have become profoundly suspicious of emotional expression, particularly public emotional expression. We think that people who are kind or solicitous out in the world are not to be trusted because they are probably being paid—or otherwise rewarded—to act that way. And because emotional expression has become commodified, Hochschild concluded,

> we have begun to place an unprecedented value on spontaneous "natural" feeling. We are intrigued by the unmanaged heart and what it can tell us. The more our emotional activities as individual emotion managers are managed by organizations, the more we tend to celebrate the life of unmanaged feeling.

In other words, the more we suspect that emotional expressions that comply with social and professional norms are not heartfelt, the more we start casting about for alternatives. If we consider the smile and impassivity of the flight attendant to be forced and untrustworthy—essentially a hired gun of pleasantness—then what of the stern authority of the news anchor or the crisp professionalism of the building inspector? If we look at it that way, cultural expectations and the norms of professionalism themselves are suspect and designed to sell us something either commercially or politically.

We start to look for a way out of the managed, corporatized feelings and interactions in order to locate some runaway "authentic" feeling. When every expression feels focus-grouped, field-tested, and commodified, it is not that surprising that we would look for that which is heartfelt, even if it is narcissistic or potentially ruinous.

This craving for the authentic has also been building for several decades now. The critic and essayist Lionel Trilling warned in a series of lectures in the spring of 1970 about the American moral turning from valuing sincerity to valuing authenticity, which he ultimately collected in his 1972 book, *Sincerity and Authenticity*. He argues that sincerity, which he defines as a type of personal integrity and commitment to values, was the glue that maintained social relationships and society itself, but that authenticity, a fealty to the innermost irreducible self, is values-neutral and has the potential to be manipulative and destructive. And yet we are attracted to its rebellion against social norms. We are attracted to the opportunity to watch the id—finally unleashed from elitist and corporatist norms—run amok.

Case in point is the 2016 election. Each time candidate Donald Trump did something outrageous, self-serving, or downright crass, we pivoted our attention, hand clasped over our mouth in some combination of horror and thrill. He said John McCain wasn't a war hero. He said he'd like to punch a protester in the face. He bragged he could shoot someone in the middle of Fifth Avenue and still not lose votes. We couldn't believe what we were hearing, and yet we kept watching. And watching some more, feeding his confidence in his own instincts and his own voice.

Voters—at least certain voters—ate it up. It was a breath of fresh air. It was a disruption to the clubby professionalism of an untrustworthy and self-serving Washington. It was a break from the droll sneering of the coastal elite. Voters awash in resentment at the phony, managed tones of institutions were swept away by Trump's audacious authenticity. Like this from a California voter, explicitly recognizing the emotional labor required of members of the clergy: "I backed Trump from the beginning. Because he calls things out. He does not allow lies to live. He just exposes things. Pastors sometimes need to be politically correct, and Donald Trump is not politically correct, and I love that about him." And this from a Florida voter: "He doesn't hold back. You get what he really believes in, even if everything that he says isn't what is the right thing exactly."

Donald Trump is most certainly not alone in a culture awash in reality TV—a construct I still cannot get my head around—and tell-all memoirs and exhortations to "just be yourself" and outraged political pundits shouting at each other on multiple channels twenty-four hours a day. Even in day-to-day interactions, there are plenty of times when we revel in displays of unvarnished ugliness, machismo, and race-baiting so long as we think such displays reflect the true feelings—at least in the moment—of the speaker or, as is so often the case, the shouter. "He," we say, "calls it like he sees it." And that is something we have come to celebrate.

Of course, the house of authenticity cannot stand, and it has probably already started to collapse in on itself. As corporations and high-stakes media ventures have watched the public cheer on that which is perceived to be authentic, no matter how crass, self-serving, or craven, those with an eye toward the profitable will have realized that "authentic expression" itself can be corporatized, repackaged, and projected.

I am a long way afield now. But at some point, the madness has to stop. How do we interrupt this cycle of purchase, mistrust, and performance? How do we wrest sincere, socially useful expressions of emotion away from the corporations and the hucksters? How do we balance our authentic selves with the care and service of others—loved ones and strangers alike? How do we show up as sane and empathetic participants in a society that feels like it has run amok?

I know I'm in a pinch here. I'm a great defender of the inner life and believe no one—the government, corporations, my mother—should have control over that great, roiling sea that exists behind our eyelids. And to argue in favor of social niceties and against untrammeled authenticity, I am getting precious close to siding with Emily Post against Carl Jung.

But I don't think the sides are that sharply drawn. I wonder what would happen if we were to reclaim what we have broadly come to call emotional labor from corporations and television producers and political consultants and then we were to decouple that work from capitalism and mass persuasion. I wonder if we might reclaim what I will from here on call "emotional work" from the market economy and re-place it firmly in the realm of freely offered gifts.

Lewis Hyde, in his beloved and groundbreaking book *The Gift*—which probably not coincidentally was published in the same year as *The Managed Heart*—argues, "It is the cardinal difference between gift and commodity exchange that a gift establishes a feeling-bond between two people, while the sale of a commodity leaves no necessary connection." He suggests that it is our burden, and perhaps our joy, to discern between those products that can and should be exchanged in an open market and those human offerings that must be freely given and accepted. *The Gift* is a beacon for artists who struggle with the question of commodification and valuation of their work, but it can also inform us as we consider the consequences of corporatized emotion. As Hyde describes it, commodities can cross boundaries, both formal and informal, but a true gift either erases the boundary or transforms itself into a commodity. As he sums it up: "*Logos*-trade draws the boundaries, *eros*-trade erases it."

At this late point, perhaps it makes sense to define exactly what I value and want to preserve in the realm of emotional work. And though I know that some of the socially expected restraint (of, say, anger) and projection (of, say, friendliness) can be toxic to the one expected to do the work, I still—for myself—value emotional work broadly rather than narrowly. I am thinking of all sorts of private gestures that are "not my job": smiling at an elder, holding open a door, stepping back from a bar so that someone else may order, remembering a birthday, scheduling my daughters' dentist appointments, noticing when a colleague seems down, writing a thank-you card, baking cookies for a class party, welcoming a new family into the neighborhood. But I am also thinking of a whole host of more public-facing tasks that might recivilize our shared civic life—listening to someone I disagree with, admitting when I am wrong, bearing witness to injustice, earnestly explaining my own experience, keeping my mouth closed when it's time to hear from someone else, examining my own conscience, asking the next question.

I am also keenly interested in the tension Hyde identifies for public officials living among us. He frames the issue like this: "We want such people to become a part of their community, but we do not want them to be beholden to one particular element. Is a policeman who accepts an apple from a greengrocer an extortionist? Is he a lackey of the grocery trade, or is he merely accepting and expressing his connection to the group he serves?" That line between connection and favoritism is a fraught one. On the one hand, we have a long-habituated expectation that our public officials are impartial and approach each of us on our individual merits. On the other hand, we know deep down that by denying the bonds of friendship or affection or community, we are isolating powerful members of our society in an unnatural way, setting them up to disappoint us when they seek or are offered human connection outside professionalized norms and expectations.

All of these questions make ethical and emotional boundary-drawing more complex rather than less. Maybe we should simply stop framing these habits of the heart—as Alexis de Tocqueville called them—as jobs at all. Maybe we can purge some of the expectation and toxicity by resisting cooptation by capitalism. Maybe the decision to live in ambiguity is in and of itself emotional work. Susan Sontag was once asked about the work of a writer. She replied, "Several things. Love words, agonize over sentences. And pay attention to the world."

Poet and essayist Lia Purpura puts it like this:

> The act of creating metaphors is a spiritual act. . . . There are so many silent, invisible tethers between people, between people and objects, between objects and ideas, and metaphors uncover all the invisible ways we are connected and all the invisible ways that surprise us. They force you to see things in others or in "the other" that you had not seen. That act of rebirth is exactly what metaphors are working on,

constant rebirth of attention, of recognition, constant rebirth of your capacity for aligning yourself with another creature, another person.

Emotional work, all of it. And none of it directly commodified.

When we reframe the work of paying attention and loving and agonizing as essential human tasks, central to what we do to live in—and make sense of—a broken time on a stressed and reeling planet, the fog of confusion begins to lift. Yes, there is the risk that Arlie Hochschild warns us about—the risk that our actual felt emotions can begin to blur with the emotional actions that we take on behalf of others. And yet to take that fear too seriously assumes that our inner emotional state is more fixed than it actually is. Perhaps I speak only for myself and Walt Whitman when I say it, but the inner life contains multitudes and is mercurial and ever-changing. As psychiatrist and Holocaust survivor Viktor Frankl spent his life saying: "Everything can be taken from a man but one thing: the last of the human freedoms—to choose one's attitude in any given set of circumstances, to choose one's own way."

And for me, that is where the impulses of the inner life and outer acts of grace might come together. It is not my *job*, but it is my choice to seek to consider the lives and needs of those around me, and it is my choice to throw my inner resources into the society where I find myself. It is my choice to choose generosity, to choose tenderness, and even to do things that I am not paid or expected to do in order to make my household or my neighborhood or my country work a little more smoothly and a little more humanistically. As my friend Eric Liu puts it, "we must not detach" from our idealism regarding what our neighborhood or even our country *could be*. Maintaining that belief is in and of itself emotional—and noble—work.

None of this is to suggest that everyone must take on—or even value—emotional work in the same way that I do. I know that all too often those with less power are expected to emotionally coddle those with more. And I understand when people make it clear that they are not having it. Good for them. But for me, firmly re-placing emotional work in the province of gift exchange with all its generosities and mysteries defuses so much resentment. Sure, there will be some muddiness on where emotional gifts end and where expectations begin, and there will be some who are simply more suited or willing to engage in gift-based emotional work, but at least it will be a thing to contend with. A thing that we cannot shunt off on others for a few dollars or an airline ticket. A thing that makes us more emotionally mature and less susceptible to the spectacle of the id run amok. And a thing that helps make sense of the fact that once again, at 11:00 p.m. this December 23, I will be up writing last-minute holiday greetings and finishing one more batch of my grandmother's fruitcake.

March 2018

Love Does Not Boast

"NO ONE WANTS TO LIVE WITH YOU WHEN YOU HAVE ONE foot out the door." And by "no one," I guess, my ex-husband meant himself. My kids didn't seem to mind. Neither did the dog. My now-husband—who seems to be fine living with me, though the tale of how we got to this point has its own epic qualities—seems to find companionship in my skittish tendencies. He and I walk into a party knowing what time we are going to leave, having established a standing signal to be used in case one of us wants to bolt earlier than the already obscenely early agreed-upon time. Typically, there is at least a 50 percent chance we will resort to the signal.

I like to have outlets, trap doors, escape valves. I barely cross the threshold into a room without thinking about how to get out of it. When I go to a conference or a workshop, I am often making up excuses to go back to my desk before lunch the first day. And then in law school, there was a perfectly lovely dinner party at which one of my most cherished professors laughed and said to the group: "Law school is just another chapter in the book of Wendy's ambivalence." Everyone laughed knowingly. I smiled a small smile and curled a little further under my rib cage.

I tell you all this to say that ambivalence and its close relative, standoffishness, are centerpieces of my personality. In fact, I am developing a theory that standoffishness is genetically inherited. My mother is not standoffish—though I am almost certain my self-loathing around the idea derives from her—but my father definitely is. My younger daughter is a charter member of the standoffish tribe, that is, if the standoffish were capable of forming a tribe. It's heartbreaking, really. When she was younger, she would cry over being left out of sleepovers and birthday parties and walks to the coffee shop. But for me, it's easy to see: Her friends—or more accurately, her close acquaintances—thought she didn't give a damn. Touché. I wonder where she got that from.

But recently, things have started to change. And probably not for the better. I'm starting to hate my adopted and formerly cherished hometown, Portland. Outright hate it. It's not even a chapter in the Book of Ambivalence. It's a deep annoyance, a visceral loathing in a form that surprises even me. Something snapped this year. Like when your back goes out and you go from upright to dragging along the floor. Or maybe it was more like snow falling heavily until the roof collapses. Anyway, last fall, while we were working in the yard, a group of friends walked by and told us they were headed for Starky's because it was about to close. That was it. I myself had never been in Starky's, but I knew that it had been a gathering place for the gay community since the seventies. I drove by it every day, rarely failing to admire its midcentury off-the-street patio. Of course, the whole city is a gathering place for the gay community now, and Starky's is not really mine to mourn, but watching the low-slung icon crumble beneath the bulldozer while an out-of-state developer plans yet another shiny apartment building with two shops in the bottom, one of which sells house-pressed vinyl records while the other displays three unglazed vases and five size-two black dresses, I feel an essential loss.

We walk into restaurants all over our neighborhood, and they are full of people who do not look like our neighbors. And by this, I do not mean that the bars and restaurants are brimming with newly arrived immigrants speaking the world's languages. I mean nearly everyone in the restaurant has brushed her hair recently. I mean they are full of well-groomed people with expensive ripped jeans, Smartwool hoodies, and exceptionally white teeth.

Among the old-timers, there is a lot of grousing going on across Portland about how it is changing, about the price of houses, about fancy restaurants, about traffic, about hipsters, about *Portlandia*. I join right in, finding myself aroused and grumpy, regularly grumbling about white people (like me) and wealthy people (it's all relative) and hipsters, mumbling things like "This place sucks."

And yet despite my crotchetiness, I actually got ice in the belly when I heard a newly minted faculty member at a local private university proclaim, "I don't care that much about Oregon. I don't really think of it as a place. Borders around things like a state don't matter to me." Despite his very pleasant demeanor and telltale white teeth, I felt like someone had slapped me across the face. Even despite—or maybe because of—my recent haterliness, something rose up in me: I don't want to be that guy.

It wasn't just the smugness, bless his heart. It was also a kind of mirror into an ugliness I try to hide from myself. It's not just that I play hard to get, which I most certainly do, but that I am disloyal to the person or thing or place once it is "mine." Take magazines, for example. The magazines that I love reading while standing in the grocery line—I stop reading them once I subscribe to them. There are piles of magazines, many of them still inside their plastic mailing sleeves pushed to the back of the kitchen counter. Once I have committed to them, they lose their allure.

The hidey-hole that is harder and more painful to illuminate is my checkered past with relationships, one tumbling into the next, each with blurred boundaries and a trail of humiliations and wounded feelings. Even now that I have stopped with such things—rambunctious destruction can go on only so long before it becomes pathological—I still once in a while get the urge to bolt and can feel a manufactured grievance welling up in me to make my departure seem justified and right. Recognizing that morally shaky tendency makes me suspicious of the downright unpleasant disdain that I feel for my own city, for my own place on the planet.

I remember when I first moved here or, really, started spending time here regularly. I was in my early twenties and was living in and out of friends' houses and apartments as I traveled back and forth between Portland and Japan and Portland and D.C. and Portland and my parents' house a hundred miles to the south. But Portland had an unmistakable allure, one that I was not unwilling to lord over others as I flaunted my standoff-ishness toward wherever it was that I was actually living at the moment. I was moving back to Portland, making it impossible for me to commit or commit much to my new places or new friends or new lovers.

Maybe it was just because I was in that perfect, numinous age—young enough to feel like there were infinite days ahead but old enough to drive, drink, and stay out as late as I wanted. When I would come back to Portland—for weekends or holidays or summers—I loved evenings with my friends full of cheap garlicky spaghetti dinners and long conversations about books and politics and all the things we would accomplish. I loved the flouncy rose gardens in the traffic circles of my neighborhood. I loved the fact that I could see Mt. Hood as I walked home from the library or from work. I loved driving to the coast for the day with friends—just like I always imagined I would—and perusing Powell's Books and dreaming about my future family tucked into a ramshackle century-old house in a leafy neighborhood in Southeast Portland.

So now that my actual, in-the-flesh family is tucked into a ramshackle 103-year-old house in a leafy neighborhood in Southeast Portland, why am I uneasy and gritchy and casting about looking for the next right place? And—maybe more important—what are the consequences of failing to commit and of my restless desire to pack it in for greener pastures?

As I ask these questions, I can't help but return to the work of Potawatomi ecologist and writer Robin Wall Kimmerer. In her book *Braiding Sweetgrass*, she nails it:

After all these generations since Columbus, some of the wisest of Native elders still puzzle over the people who came to our shores. They look at the toll on the land and say, "The problem with these new people is that they don't have both feet on the shore. One is still on the boat. They don't seem to know whether they're staying or not."

She goes on to ask: "What happens when we truly become native to a place, when we finally make a home?" That is the question solidly before me in all its complexities. Kimmerer recognizes the risks associated with this line of questioning. She writes, "Against the backdrop of that history, an invitation to settler society to become indigenous to place feels like a free ticket to a housebreaking party. It could be read as an open invitation to take what little is left."

I don't want to be either of those people. I don't want to have one foot still on the boat, as both Kimmerer and my ex-husband suggested, but I also don't want to be a rapacious taker. I want to—I feel compelled to try to—live in a kind of humbled affection with this place, with these people. My time here is short, shorter than I want to admit, and I don't want to fall on the wrong side of the ledger. And beyond that, the very future of the planet is imperiled by our own hubris and distraction and inattention to our places.

I was particularly chastened about my own noncommittalness when I ran across an interview with the British mythologist Martin Shaw. In answer to a question about irreversible climate change, he responded:

I have not a clue whether we humans will live for another 100 or 10,000 years. We can't be sure. What matters to me is the fact we have fallen out of a very ancient love affair—a kind of dream tangle, with the earth itself. If, through our own mess, that relationship is about to end, then we need to scatter as much beauty around us as we possibly can, to send a voice, to attempt some kind of repair.

Is that it? Did I fall out of love not just with Portland or the particularities of my small life, but out of love with the world, with the earth itself? That's an indictment I am not prepared to live with. Or at least one I must correct. On the other hand, though, we hear people say the opposite all the time—I love Oregon; I love you (this crowd of twenty thousand people at a rock concert); I love America. What does that even mean when we say we love abstractly and gigantically? And how do we go so far as to love the planet, the whole planet? Are humans even capable of loving at that scale beyond a sort of vague sentimentality?

At last summer's Democratic National Convention, New Jersey senator Cory Booker exhorted us to go beyond being a nation of tolerance to become a nation of love:

> We can't devolve into a nation where our highest aspiration is that we just tolerate each other. We are not called to be a nation of tolerance. We are called to be a nation of love. Tolerance says I am just going to stomach your right to be different. That if you disappear from the face of the earth, I am no better or worse off. But love—love knows that every American has worth and value, no matter what their background, race, religion, or sexual orientation. Love recognizes that we need each other, that we as a nation are better together, that

when we are divided we are weak, we decline, yet when we
are united we are strong—invincible!

That's closer: Love focuses on interdependence and strength in
difference as well as similarity. But it still doesn't approach the
earthy, erotic love affair that Martin Shaw laments. That requires us to look further.

The Greeks tell us that there are at least five kinds of love,
maybe seven. There is *philautia*, which is an either healthy or
unhealthy form of self-love, and *ludus*, which is a flirtatious
and fundamentally unserious love. There is *pragma*, which is
just what it sounds like—practical, duty-bound, founded in
long-term interests. Think—arranged marriages or Bill and
Hillary Clinton. There is *storge*, which runs from parents to
children. And there is *philia*, which sounds something like
what Cory Booker was describing—a sort of brother- and
sisterhood of goodwill and affection—though I suspect what
he was shooting for was more like *agape*, which is the high-
water mark for Sunday school teachers everywhere. *Agape* is
said to be universal love and encompasses strangers and pit
bulls and Republicans and God. It is—as they say—not self-
ish. It is patient and kind.

That sounds good, *agape*. That must be what Senator
Booker means when he says he loves Donald Trump or what
partisans are thinking when they say they love their country.
But does *agape* just burst out in full flame, like vine maple
in October? If so, I wish I were more aflame. Honestly, I
wish my fellow citizens were, too. I like the idea of *agape*,
an all-encompassing and reliable love, but I suspect it might
need a little kindling. Maybe we need Cupid's arrow to get

us started. Maybe we need the irrational, anguished infatuation of *eros*, the intoxicating force that keeps us yearning for the beloved just long enough for the maturity of *agape* to take hold.

But what is that arrow? I am well armored, protected by brittle professionalism and superficial affability, by my half-out-the-door standoffishness.

And yet I am not immune to the erotic charms of the world, to the midnight surprise of a full moon dangling over the backyard or the magic of an unexpected snowfall, to the hilarity of a dog and a daughter chasing each other across the soccer field. Somehow, I am reminded of the poem by Turkish poet Nazim Hikmet, "Things I Didn't Know I Loved," and its accelerating affections. The poem begins the year before Hikmet's death:

> it's 1962 March 28th
> I'm sitting by the window on the Prague-Berlin train
> night is falling

He starts out begrudgingly, cranky and suspicious of his own motives:

> I never knew I liked
> night descending like a tired bird on a smoky wet plain
> I don't like
> comparing nightfall to a tired bird

> I didn't know I loved the earth
> can someone who hasn't worked the earth love it

I've never worked the earth
it must be my only Platonic love

But then he picks up speed and ferocity, recalling his love of
rivers, and the sky—cloudy or clear—and the trees in Moscow
and roads (even the asphalt kind) and the three red carnations
friends sent him in prison and stars and snow and the clouds
until he ends here:

the train plunges on through the pitch-black night
I never knew I liked the night pitch-black
sparks fly from the engine
I didn't know I loved sparks
I didn't know I loved so many things and I had to wait until
    sixty
to find it out sitting by the window on the Prague-Berlin
    train
watching the world disappear as if on a journey of no return

Maybe it is my age—nearer to sixty than twenty—but is
it possible that it is the brink itself, the cusp of death and destruction that could return us to infatuation, to *eros*, to a full-on
Venusian swoon? It's not just recognition that I will die but that
the planet itself is in a life-threatening spiral that imperils everything I have and will ever love. Does that snap us to attention? Is that the arrow?

That said, I am who I am. So far, I can't muster the ecstasy
of a Martin Shaw–style infatuation. The ambivalence runs deep.
This is a place I need to keep working, keep peeling back the

layers of reserve, keep setting down my purse inside the front door. This is the place that I need to put on my high heels and brightest lipstick and go looking for seduction. This is the place I need to loosen my breastplate and invite the arrow to land.

March 2017

The Sacred and Profane
of Vote-by-Mail

VOTING IN THE UNITED STATES IS A NUMINOUS ACT, shimmering between the quotidian and the mythic. On one hand, there is nothing more ordinary than sharpening a number-two pencil and then blacking out a few tiny circles. And yet we Americans valorize voting as the bedrock act of citizenship— the act that separates us from totalitarians one graphite mark at a time.

We know how hard-won the vote was for many Americans as we recall the murder of Jimmie Lee Jackson by an Alabama state trooper and the beating near to death of Congressman John Lewis on the Edmund Pettus Bridge. And Elizabeth Cady Stanton, though she devoted her life to the cause, didn't live to see women gain the right to vote. Looking abroad, we were seared by images of Afghan women stepping outside polling places with purple-inked forefingers, a bodily mark of the right they had gained and then exercised. As Congressman Lewis put it, "The vote is precious. It's almost sacred."

So when my home state of Oregon went to an all vote-by-mail system in 1998, I was ambivalent. Of course, I want to remove barriers to voting. I want folks with multiple jobs or disabilities or small children to have a way to participate that does not create a tremendous burden on them or their families.

In practice, though, voting feels less sacred than ever before. Ballots arrive two weeks before the election, along with pizza coupons and bills and offers for new credit cards. At our house, we shuffle the ballots from pile to pile until my husband and I finally get around to filling them out, sometimes together and sometimes separately. They'll sit around for days, but out of some insistent idea of how things should be, I refuse to actually put my ballot in the U.S. mail. Instead, I wait until Election Day to drop my ballot in a mailbox outside county election headquarters. Even so, voting feels much more like paying the gas bill than like a solemn reaffirmation of citizenship.

I miss waking up on Election Day with butterflies in my stomach. I miss saying hello to my friends and neighbors in the hallway of the elementary school and chatting with the gray-haired volunteers and wearing the "I voted" sticker all day. I miss the sound of the curtain rings pulling across the metal rod as I close the red-and-blue-striped drapes behind me. I miss acting out my citizenship in public, though the final act is at least ostensibly in private.

I suppose it is time to make an admission. I am a Catholic. And I remain so—despite my hostility to the institutional

Church as a protector of power and patriarchy—for a very specific reason: a deep craving for shared ritual. I am a believer at an almost cellular level in the importance of creating sacred occasions to drag ourselves out of our private experiences, to connect to the past and the future, and to remind ourselves of our aspirations to be better. I believe that the repetition of words and gestures in the presence of friends and strangers renews a sense of shared identity and communal obligation.

Although I am an extreme case, a need for ritual is not some quirk unique to me. Ritual is central to meaning-making, to ennobling our concept of ourselves and our communities. As mythologist Joseph Campbell put it, "A ritual is the enactment of a myth. And, by participating in the ritual, you are participating in the myth." For Americans, voting is one of the very few civic rituals that we—in mass numbers—actually perform ourselves. We observe a fair number of civic rituals: political conventions, the State of the Union Address, state funerals, even parades. In each of those cases, though we are invited to watch, most of us are not asked to participate ourselves. It's sort of like watching church on television.

Voting is different. The mythology behind the ritual of voting is one of shared power and responsibility. It is one of an earnest and informed citizenry striving for the common good. By taking it out of the public sphere and placing it on my kitchen counter, it just feels like one more private task to be crammed into an already hectic life. It feels like filling out a field trip permission form.

I think it would matter less to me if public life had not become so degraded in other ways. Lying is de rigueur. The State of the Union is an opportunity to parade partisan preferences and exploit the fears of a deflated nation. Even Memorial Day and Thanksgiving—the great civic rituals that came out of the Civil War—have become mostly opportunities to take advantage of department-store sales on barbeques and laptops. As Joseph Campbell quipped to Bill Moyer three decades ago, "If you want to find out what it means to have a society without any rituals, read the *New York Times*."

At this point, I'd just like to walk into a voting booth, pull the lever, smile at a stranger on my way out, and get my damn sticker. I'd like—for one day—to feel like we could be better tomorrow than we are today.

My friend Phil Keisling, Oregon's former secretary of state and a national leader in the vote-by-mail movement, calls my resistance—very gently—"misguided sentimentality." He argues that the essence of democracy does not reside in an anachronistic ritual but rather in maximum participation. He argues—persuasively—that vote-by-mail is a much fairer system and that Oregon and Washington, the only two exclusively vote-by-mail states, consistently post some of the highest voter turnouts, particularly in primary and off-year elections.

Of course, this makes me feel like a privileged brat or a granny pining for the rotary-dial phone or the eccentric neighbor who swears she prefers the metallic taste of well water. Who am I to miss my little sticker when there are mothers with four kids working two jobs who don't have time to go chat with volunteers from the League of Women Voters? Who am I to oppose a democratic innovation that strengthens self-governance? As Phil patiently suggested to me, "Now that we have worked on participation, we can create new rituals."

Indeed, after fourteen years, people *have* created new

rituals. Some people have dessert with friends and fill out their ballots together. Many people vote with their children, answering questions and puzzling through the issues as a family. And many, many of my friends have created tender moments with their sweethearts over their mail-in ballots.

But those are *private* rituals. I love private rituals. I believe in lovers and parents and old friends anticipating and repeating gestures that mean something to them. They enact and reenact private myths that undoubtedly provide social glue and shared meaning.

But what I am mourning is the *public* ritual—a gesture enacting a sense of civic duty, an act of common purpose fulfilled together whether we know each other or not. In 1966, sociologist Robert Neelly Bellah published a widely cited and somewhat controversial article titled "Civil Religion in America," in which he emphasized that "civil religion, including invocations of god and civil rituals," provides a "transcendent goal for the political process." As public rituals erode—even in simple ways like eliminating polling stations and voting booths—I wonder what might be left of our shared sense of transcendence.

Maybe Phil is right and I am trying too hard to make sacred an act that has long since been desacralized. Maybe elections don't deserve that kind of solemn observance anymore. At best, elections have become transactional—individuals are called on to calculate which candidate or measure benefits them the most personally and then vote accordingly. We are asked to wear the familiar and well-worn T-shirt of the consumer and rarely—if ever—to dust off the Sunday hat of citizenship. At worst, elections have become spectacles—sideshows distorted by money and bare-knuckled power plays and petty distractions. Nothing is out of bounds. It is expected that candidates and advocates and ordinary citizens—for that matter—will lie, defame, and manipulate to win. If that's the case, then there is no sacred spark to fan.

And by that, I don't mean to suggest that we should eliminate vote-by-mail or widespread absentee voting or early voting or same-day registration or motor-voter or any other innovation designed to maximize participation or reduce burdens on the vulnerable. The logical response to concentrated power and a system marinated in money is massive, popular participation. One bulwark against well-funded and cynical manipulation is to make voting as easy and simple as possible, felling every conceivable barrier, even the ones that whisper to our civic angels.

My attitude about this is not so different from my feelings about the Church, tarnished by greed and entrenched power and callous abuse of the innocent. These days, it feels a little bombed-out at the center, so when I have the choice, I most often opt for my private ritual of strong coffee and the Sunday *Times*. But I still love the *idea* of kneeling with my fellow parishioners in the church of Dante, even if I don't do it that often anymore.

Yes, on the first Tuesday after the first Monday in November, maybe I should give unto Caesar what is Caesar's. Maybe I should celebrate what is fast, convenient, and grimly participatory. Maybe I should bake a pie and hunker down with my family. Maybe I should smother with a pillow that last whisper of misplaced sentimentality and get out my stamps.

But I won't.

In the same way that I will show up to Mass today—All Saints' Day—to sing the Litany of Saints with my neighbors,

I will carry my ballot around in my purse until next Tuesday. I will recall the struggle and sacrifice of Jimmie Lee Jackson and John Lewis and Elizabeth Cady Stanton. I will stop for my latte and walk down to Multnomah County Elections Headquarters. I will greet the folks I meet in the coffee shop and on the sidewalk. I will breathe deep the bustle of occasion. I will drop my ballot into the puce mailbox outside on the sidewalk and whisper to myself, *Wendy Willis has voted.*

November 2012

I'd Have to Cry These Wounds to Mourn for Us

THIS PAST SUMMER, I SPENT THE WEEK OF THE REPUBLI-can National Convention in a workshop focused on racial justice and healing. This is not a workshop for the faint of heart. It asks you to dig deep into your own muck and then dredge it all out for forty strangers to take a look at. One of my friends—who warned me before I went—calls it "feelings camp." But it's the sort of place where someone like me, whose job and disposition involve fretting over the future of the Republic, might find herself during a sunny July week.

By day, I witnessed a mixed-race, mixed-age group of Americans show up and try to be better. To be better for themselves and for one another. There was anger and sulking and ugly-crying mixed with a lot of laughter, both anxious and joyful. By night, I guiltily wallowed in televised coverage of the most craven of American political traditions—the nominating convention.

The morning after Donald Trump accepted the nomination of the Republican Party, I showed up at the training jangly and exhausted. I was worn down from nearly a week of crying in public and from the brick-hot rage being disgorged from the podium of one of our major political parties. The trainer (a woman for whom by this point we would all have walked through fire) sensed the fatigue and distraction in the room. So she finally stood up and said, "Here's the deal—and I am especially talking to you white people—you need to love Donald Trump."

I set my coffee cup down between my feet. "What in the actual hell?" I mouthed to my co-worker.

"No, I'm serious," she went on. "People don't act like that for no reason. He's yours to figure out, and I guarantee there is some particular suffering at the root of all that anger."

I've been mulling that challenge nearly every day since, trying to imagine both how I could conceivably love Donald Trump and what could possibly be the suffering at the heart of the poisonous and patently false rhetoric being spewed by him and—even more disturbingly—by his whipped-up followers. Most of the time, my imagination fails me.

But I also suspect that failure may be at least part of the problem. To the extent that presidential elections can tell us anything about the American character, this one seems to be revealing a stunning atrophying of the imagination.

The core assumption on which a representative democracy is built is that, while an elected official cannot share the precise experiences of all her constituents, she can and should imagine herself into their particular and varied life circumstances.

The larger the number of constituents, the greater the need for a broad and rich imagination. And the greater the need for a cultivated sense of empathy.

The president—for example—needs to be able to imagine the lives of both the injured logger hooked on opioids and his wife who can no longer tolerate the volatility of the home. The president needs to imagine himself or herself into the life of a young African American man who is terrified he will be shot by the police and that of the white patrol officer who fears for her life every day. The president needs to imagine the terror and desperation of parents who pack up their small children and flee violence in their home country and the Rust Belt textile worker who is afraid he will never work again. Because presidents—or for that matter mayors and city council members—can never be all those things, it is essential that they be able to empathetically consider the circumstances of millions of strangers living their own lives and enduring their own particular forms of pain.

That's a tall order. After all, we ordinary citizens and those we choose to represent us come to the public square already bearing our own scars and carrying our own suffering. And now we are asking our elected officials—and ourselves—to take on more hardship and need. We are being asked to imagine the suffering of people we don't know and strongly suppose we don't like. In that struggle, I am reminded of "I Just Missed the Bus and I'll Be Late for Work" by Chilean poet Ariel Dorfman, in this translation by Edith Grossman:

> I'd have to piss through my eyes to cry for you,
> salivate, sweat, sigh through my eyes,

I'd have to waterfall
I'd have to wine
I'd have to die like crushed grapes
through my eyes,
cough up vultures spit green silence
and shed a dried-up skin
no good to animals
no good for a trophy
I'd have to cry these wounds
this war
to mourn for us

That kind of searing bodily empathy begins in the imagination, and it is relentless work. I fear we may be out of practice.

If this election cycle is any indicator, however, it seems our collective dark imagination is in fine working order. Many of us don't have any trouble projecting evil motives and nefarious plans on immigrants and Muslims and people in dozens of countries around the globe. And others of us feel fully entitled to sneer at the pitifulness of folks we have decided are uneducated or ignorant or bigoted. But this campaign has also revealed just how weak our brighter empathetic imagination has become. The rhetoric of many—if not most—of the candidates has embraced black-and-white thinking and an us-versus-them ethos poisonous to a flexible, empathetic spirit. The name-calling, the otherizing, the appeals to the fight-or-flight levers of the reptile parts of our brains all impede us from being able to get outside ourselves and beyond our basest fears.

This is a global disease. The current brand of populism, both in the United States and around the world, is rooted in individual grievance and is suspicious of collective action and the institutions designed to support it. And I fear it is not by happenstance. Demagogues gain by breathlessly warning us there are barbarians threatening our families and homes and ways of life. Atomization—even atomization leading to an angry but diffuse mob—is preferable to empathy and understanding if you are seeking to maintain power and wealth.

But here's the thing: we can't just blame the powerful or the greedy. The rest of us are also responsible for this ugly state of public imagination and the vulnerability to demagoguery and tyranny that comes with it. Representative democracy has requirements for us, too. In the same way that our elected officials are called to imagine themselves into our lives, we are called to consider their lives as well.

Almost every time I take a Monday-morning flight from my outpost in Oregon to the East Coast, I run into one of our members of Congress flying back to Washington. Yes, it's their job, but try to imagine that reality. Seven Oregonians fly three thousand miles nearly every Thursday night or Friday morning to try to maintain some semblance of a family life while juggling constituents with sometimes grievous problems—before flying back across the country to try to represent our interests in a fractured and fractious institution.

And that's the least of it. Imagine making life-or-death decisions for American service members every single day. Or in these times of constrained budgets, imagine trying to decide whether to cut services for the elderly or the disabled or the young. Or to use an extreme example from history:

Put yourself in President Truman's position as he weighed whether to use the atomic bomb to end the war with Japan. Even decisions made to try to save the country from catastrophe sometimes carry with them politically fatal consequences. As Vice President Joe Biden said about the administration's decision to promote and support the economic bailout of the financial system: "Voting to support TARP in the Congress was like . . . putting rattlesnakes in people's kitchens. . . . I mean—because the very people they blamed for the problem were being bailed out."

When we fail to consider the burdens and responsibilities and no-win decisions facing those we elect, we are unable—or unwilling—to imagine the pressures, the sleeplessness, the terror and agony of making a mistake. Instead, it is all too easy to get swept up in our own grievances, unrealistically expecting perfection and polish and demanding entertainment in the form of witty sound bites. And then the whole undertaking of representative government becomes a partisan game rather than a shared and flawed human activity for which we are all responsible.

The 2016 presidential campaign has brimmed over with ugliness and divisiveness that could take us years—maybe decades—to recover from. But the great thing about the imagination is that it's an internal state. Each of us can start there, within ourselves. Maybe we can cultivate a practice of standing in one another's shoes, including the shoes of those who seek to represent us. Maybe we can imagine ourselves into the life of a neighbor from the opposite political party or a member of Congress or even a presidential candidate.

Even after all these weeks of mulling, I can't honestly say I love Donald Trump. I don't know that I ever will. But I do try to imagine the burdens he seeks to take on, and those are heavy ones indeed.

October 2016

FERLINGHETTI'S PERFUME

Reckoning with the Bros

Donald Trump, Robert Bly, and
Swimming in the Sea of Grief

THERE ARE DARK FORCES ROILING BENEATH THE SUR-face of American life. Along with nearly everyone from my side of the political spectrum and many from the other, I am wringing my hands as I watch thousands of enraged voters turning up for Make America Great Again rallies and candidates competing for who can be cruelest to the most vulnerable people and grown men standing behind podiums behaving like they just learned a naughty word out on the schoolyard. It's not just the political entertainment class that is acting out, either. There are shouting matches and fisticuffs and rhetorical venom exchanged between friends and co-workers and ordinary folks standing next to each other at parades as well as at political rallies. Meanwhile, earlier this winter, armed, flag-waving men took over a wildlife refuge here in my own state, making proclamations about returning public lands to the people and a revolution to resist tyranny.

Meanwhile people like me respond with what we think are sharp policy questions: How exactly does Donald Trump plan to force Mexico to pay to build a two-thousand-mile wall? What are the nitty-gritty details of how he intends to help Americans make "much more money" rather than increase the minimum wage? Why were the Bundys and their fellow occupiers trying to force a rural county to take over 190,000 acres it has no ability or desire to manage? What is the most tactical way to battle ISIS without bombing innocent families and children?

But it's evident something else is going on here. Something that has very little to do with policy. The other night, a friend said she feels like the id is run amok. I prefer Jung to Freud, arguing that the unexamined shadow is emerging from the unconscious. Either way, it seems as if we are taking to the public square to air our basest and most vicious impulses. I just wish Joseph Campbell were around with his mythologist's eye to interpret all this for us.

It was in that frame of mind that I went to see Haydn Reiss's new documentary about the life and work of the poet Robert Bly. The film begins at the 1968 National Book Award ceremony with Bly denouncing the war in Vietnam and turning over his $1,000 award check—which he undoubtedly could have used about then, since he was living on a farm in Minnesota raising a young family—to some kid he found at the office of the draft resistance movement. As he put it:

> As Americans, we have always wanted the life of feeling
> without the life of suffering. We long for pure light, constant

victory. We have always wanted to avoid suffering, and therefore we are unable to live in the present. But our hopes for a life of pure light are breaking up. So many of the books nominated this year—Mr. Kozol's on education in the slums, Mr. Styron's, Mr. Rexroth's, Mr. Mumford's, Miss Levertov's, Mr. Merwin's—tell us from now on we will have to live with grief and defeat.

Right. That's it, isn't it? We Americans have tied our fate to the galloping horse of capitalism with one rein and the rampaging bull of empire with the other. We proclaim our faith in unlimited growth and a new car every two years and each generation doing better than the last and viral democracy and American exceptionalism and a cheerful liberty that is unburdened by recollections of slavery or Indian removal or Japanese internment. And maybe it isn't quite turning out like we'd hoped; maybe we aren't able to cheat the human condition and the limitations of a stressed planet. Maybe we have lost a few wars in a row and are carrying a huge debt and are finding that the wealthy are getting wealthier and that good fortune is not trickling down to improve the lives of Americans from coast to coast. Maybe—at least in part—we've been telling ourselves a big fat lie. And rather than turning inward to face our disappointment and suffering and grief, we're just pitching an old-fashioned fit. We're railing at our parents and the government and big corporations and the horse they all rode in on. And here Bly was talking about it from before the time I could walk.

Haydn Reiss—who appeared at the screening I attended—said he had hoped to make a "legacy document" to share Bly's life and work with future generations. And the film succeeds in giving us an overview of the whole Bly. From the opening at the National Book Awards ceremony, the movie returns to the farm of his birth and walks through his life in more or less chronological order, interspersing footage of Bly in action with interviews of a who's who of American poetry—Edward Hirsch, Philip Levine, Donald Hall, Jane Hirshfield, Tracy K. Smith.

My own relationship with Robert Bly has been complex. I first read him as an undergraduate, though I am not sure why since almost certainly I was not assigned *This Tree Will Be Here for a Thousand Years* in any literature course I ever took. I suspect I was nipping from the secret stash of used poetry collections that kept me alive and at least partially intact while I wrestled with schoolwork and romances and the new identities I tried on every few weeks. But I am almost positive that *This Tree* was the first I read—and probably ever heard—of Robert Bly.

After seeing the film a few weeks ago, I returned to that first book and every other Bly book lying around our house— *Loving a Woman in Two Worlds*, *The Man in the Black Coat Turns*, *The Morning Glory*, *Silence in the Snowy Fields*, and of course *The Light Around the Body*, the book for which he won the 1968 National Book Award. I had already been poking my way through the cantankerous essays in *American Poetry: Wildness and Domesticity*, and I finally got around to reading *The Sibling Society*.

I know that some of the other collections are more acclaimed, but returning to *This Tree Will Be Here for a Thousand Years* jerked me right back to my nineteen-year-old self, reading poems and choking down espresso in a campus coffeehouse. I was a serious kid—serious about grades, serious about succeeding, serious about being good. I was a political science major with some moonbeam longings, though I did my best to keep those mostly to myself. And while I loved the rough-and-tumble of politics and the adrenaline rush that went with it, I still longed for connection to the inner life that only literature can deliver. So while by day I railed against the injustices of colonialism and imperialism, by night I read poems that tapped into an unseen world in which the rules of materialism were askance and a feral intelligence reigned over the kingdom, poems like this one:

There are women we love whom we never see again.
They are chestnuts shining in the rain.
Moths hatched in winter disappear behind books.
Sometimes when you put your hand into a hollow tree
you touch the dark places between the stars.
Human war has parted messengers from another planet,
who cross back to each other at night,
going through slippery valleys, farmyards where the rain
     has washed out all the tracks,
and when we walk there, with no guide, saddened, in the
     dark
we see above us glowing the fortress made of ecstatic blue
     stone.

The introduction to *This Tree* must have been just as stunning to the nineteen-year-old me who was trying to make her way in the late-twentieth-century world while still loving it in the peculiar way of a twelfth-century ecstatic nun or a Druid as it was to the middle-aged me when I reread it this week. This, this must have scraped close to the bone:

Many ancient Greek poems, on the other hand, suggest that human beings and the "green world" share a consciousness. Each of the poems that follow contains an instant sometimes twenty seconds long, sometimes longer, when I was aware of two separate energies: my own consciousness, which is insecure, anxious, massive, earthbound, persistent, cunning, hopeful; and a second consciousness which is none of these things. The second consciousness has a melancholy tone, the tear inside the stone, what Lucretius calls "the tears of thing," an energy circling downward, felt often in autumn or moving slowly around apple trees or stars.

When I first read it, I must have thought: *Robert Bly was fifty-three years old when he published this book. He is startled by snow and amazed by horses and plow furrows. Surely there must be hope for me.* I was desperate to make contact with—and then ride the contrails of—the unseen world. And Bly was right there as my traveling companion, goading me and apparently all of American poetry along with me, though I didn't know it at the time.

I suppose I fell head over heels for Bly because he was—as Edward Hirsch put it in the film—a "citizen and a mystic" who was both excavating the deep interior and speaking out against American policy in Central America. And I was desperate to believe that it was possible to do both things over the long haul.

Bly warned in the movie, "It's hard to live in metaphor in the modern world." And he elaborated in his 1997 book, *The Sibling Society*, "The increasingly hurried and harried college education that comes before business means that many men and women graduate without ever having any experience of the 'other worlds,' or of deeper meanings."

Damn straight. Though at nineteen, I had no idea just how much harder it would get. It's actually relatively easy to linger in the world of metaphor when all you have to do is feed your mind, sit in coffee shops until 2:00 a.m., and fret over life on the other side of the higher education moat. It gets a lot harder when there are mortgages and ballet recitals and overflowing laundry baskets and idiosyncratic bosses and check engine lights and hungry dogs and immunization records and editorial deadlines and mammograms and school photos to worry about.

But I didn't know that then. All I knew is that I was the girl who was interested in both folkloric magic and pressuring the university to divest its endowment from South Africa. And I mooned after a poet who could both write this:

> "Living" means eating up particles of death,
>   as a child picks up crumbs from around the table.
> "Floating" means letting the crumbs fall behind you on
>   the path.
> To live is to rush ahead eating up your own death,
>   Like an endgate, open, hurrying into the night.

and call out The Man—in all his forms—over the war in Vietnam:

> What has the book industry done to end the war? Nothing. What have our universities done to end the war? Nothing. What have our museums, like the Metropolitan, done? Nothing. What has my own publisher, Harper & Row, done to help end the war? Nothing. In an age of gross and savage crimes by legal governments, the

institutions will have to learn responsibility, learn to take their part in preserving the nation, and take their risk by committing acts of disobedience.

So when Bly published *Iron John* in 1990—a book I have still not read but reportedly is a mythological celebration of masculinity—I took it pretty hard. Given that the entirety of Western culture felt like a mythological celebration of masculinity, not only was I not that interested, but I was disgusted by the whole enterprise. And one of the delightful things about Reiss's movie was that I got to feel angry and annoyed all over again. At the time *Iron John* came out, I was outraged. I had taken Bly to be an equal-opportunity tender of the soul. I saw him as a magician, a shaman, a portal to the unseen world, and it never really occurred to me that this pied piper of the archetypal wasn't talking to me. I didn't realize that this alluring version of human existence was just for the guys and that I was supposed to watch from the bleachers, like so many other times in a young woman's life.

After *Iron John* came out, I left Bly for dead. By that time, I had had plenty of experience with men celebrating their manliness at my expense, sometimes at my great expense. So I rolled my eyes at the spectacle of dentists and tax lawyers binding up their psychic wounds with red ribbon and drumming in the forest. And though I never have been able to make myself read the thing, I enthusiastically joined in the feminist critique that went something like this: *Enlightened and mythologically informed as it might be, patriarchy still sucks.* After that, I never went back to those magical poems in *This Tree Will Be Here for a Thousand Years* or *Silence in the Snowy Fields* with any enthusiasm or particular attention. I completely missed Bly's ghazal era and the late poems honoring Chinese masters.

So I was puzzled by my own reaction to the packed Bly retrospective I attended last April in Minneapolis. Tony Hoagland, Marie Howe, and Jill Bialosky were on the panel, flanked by musicians and upstaged by a magician (this was, after all, a celebration of Robert Bly). To my surprise, Bly and his wife, Ruth, turned up and sat right in the front row. At that point, Bly was eighty-eight years old and had reportedly been suffering from Alzheimer's disease or some other memory disorder for more than a few years. He was as tall and imposing as ever, but bonier, thinner, less electric. After the tributes were complete, the moderator surprised the room with the announcement that Bly felt up to reading a few poems. So he turned his chair around and read poems from his most recent book, *Like the New Moon I Will Live My Life*. As he read the poems peppered with his trademark asides ("I don't know what that means, but it sounds good, doesn't it?"), there he was. The voice, the quickness, the snowy exterior world juxtaposed with deep dives into the murky interior. As soon as he started reading, I started to cry. And I didn't let up until well after we had walked out of the crowded lecture hall.

My attitude was a little confused by the time I attended the screening of *A Thousand Years of Joy*. Of course, there were a lot of older dudes featured in the film, from both the poetry world and the men's movement (though Jane Hirshfield and Tracy K. Smith and Louise Erdrich also made appearances in it), and there were a lot of older dudes in the audience as well. And I did feel annoyed—all over again—at what I guess we are calling the mythopoetic men's movement. But this time, even that huge diversion in Bly's career made me feel a little tender toward him.

He and his peculiar form of celebratory masculinity didn't really seem like much of a threat in the end, and at least he swung for the fences. At least he believed enough in the tools of poetry and myth and storytelling to try to connect American men to the interior world despite the fact that he subjected himself to both ridicule and rancor inside the poetry world.

And overwhelmingly, both last spring and later in the movie theater, I felt grief. I felt grief for Bly gripped by the nasty talons of Alzheimer's or aging or whatever it is. I felt grief for me that the years have passed so fast since I was that earnest coed. I felt grief that we are doing no better at staying out of wars and protecting the people and creatures of this planet than we were when Bly first started sounding the alarm. And I felt grief for a country that continues to be disconnected from the inner life and the wisdom that it might offer in the face of hate-filled rhetoric and demagoguery.

The fact is, grief is my closest familiar these days. I grieve for some idealized innocence that has never existed for my children. I grieve that they are one day closer to being out in the world than they were yesterday. I grieve for the fact that racial justice seems further away than ever and that I feel increasingly unable to be a force for good in that fight. I grieve for the fact that my paved-over neighborhood was once the habitat for elk and gray wolves and old-growth fir. And—this is the one that threatens to drag me into the undertow—I grieve over the fact that an entire generation, including me, has been so careless and greedy and addicted to convenience that we have likely doomed the planet and all of its inhabitants to a bleak and catastrophic future. At this point, I am awash in grief that could, and sometimes does, overwhelm all other emotions.

That's the rub, isn't it? That's the difference in returning to Bly as a middle-aged woman rather than encountering him for the first time as an undergraduate. Then I was such a wound-up ball of longing and fear that all I could seek was hope and encouragement. And I found some romantic version of it. But Bly, he knew it was about grief all along. As he said—all those years ago—we are in an era in which we must live in grief and defeat. And that's the place we're unwilling to go as a culture. It is inconsistent with our televised vision of ourselves as "winners" and as "the greatest nation on earth." And, honestly, it's just too scary.

So the unconscious erupts. We will do anything not to feel swamped in defeat and grief and hopelessness and guilt and shame, so we fight back with rancor and hatred and ugliness. But if we listen honestly to the voices of that other world, the one Bly has spent his life tuning his ears for—in ways sublime and ridiculous—we know we have companions in our suffering:

> Come with me into those things that have felt this despair
> for so long—
> Those removed Chevrolet wheels that howl with a terrible
> loneliness,
> Lying on their backs in the cindery dirt, like men drunk,
> and naked,
> Staggering off down a hill at night to drown at last in the
> pond.
> Those shredded inner tubes abandoned on the shoulders of
> thruways,
> Black and collapsed bodies, that tried and burst,
> And were left behind;

And the curly steel shavings, scattered about on garage
    benches,
Sometimes still warm, gritty when we hold them,
Who have given up, and blame everything on the government,
And those roads in South Dakota that feel around in the
    darkness . . .

Unlike Bly, I am not inclined to dwell in the world of grief forever, but I know we have to pass through and we might have to
stay a good long while. But Bly reminds us that, for now, our
whole world lives under a sheen of grief, and if we are willing,
we can see clearly here, too, and not feel so alone.

May 2016

An All-or-Nothing Gamble

Václav Havel and His Spiritual Revolution

"MICHAEL," WHISPERED FORMER CZECH PRESIDENT Václav Havel to his now-biographer Michael Zantovsky when they met for the last time, "I am a ruin." At that point, Havel and Zantovsky had known each other for more than thirty years. Zantovsky had covered Havel as a journalist for Reuters, then collaborated with him during the run-up to the 1989 Velvet Revolution that overthrew the communist regime, and finally served as Havel's press secretary for the first two of his four terms as president. In his introduction to *Havel: A Life*, Zantovsky anticipates the critique that he is being self-serving or indulging in sentimental hagiography and—as Havel himself might have done—openly questions his fitness to serve as Havel's biographer. As he put it: "My own relationship to Havel can best be described by a word I use with the utmost reluctance.... Being in love with the subject of one's biography is not necessarily the best qualification for writing it."

And yet it is just that proximity—that intimacy and affection, that love—that makes Zantovsky's version of Havel's life unique in the world of political biography and that drew me to it. Václav Havel has long been ensconced in my own personal hall of heroes, but now he lives in the nation's as well. Last fall, a bronze-and-gold bust was unveiled in Statuary Hall in the U.S. Capitol, making Havel one of only four foreign leaders to be included in the Rotunda. There was rare bipartisan agreement on Havel's worthiness to be honored—House Speaker John Boehner lauded him as a lion in the defeat of communism and Minority Leader Nancy Pelosi valorized him as a warrior for human rights.

Indeed, it is difficult not to romanticize the Havel story. Though he was born into a well-to-do family, those very privileges put him on the outs with the communist authorities from the moment they took over postwar Czechoslovakia. He was labeled a "bourgeois element" and was denied even a traditional high school education. Following night school and a stint in the military, Havel fell in with a group of writers and artists, and began to publish poems, essays, and plays. In 1963, he wrote *The Garden Party*, an allegorical farce that became the hottest theater ticket in town. From 1963 until 1965, hordes of young people waited in line for tickets, some of them seeing the play more than a dozen times.

The Garden Party and several of the plays that followed were well received not only in Prague but also in theaters throughout the West, raising Havel's profile abroad and giving him a small but steady source of income. While his reputation as an artist grew, so did his visibility as a resister to communist Czechoslovakia's restrictions on free thought and expression. Though the 1968 Prague Spring and resulting Soviet crackdown were the focus of the world, Havel's true breaking point came a few years later—in 1976—when members of the rock band Plastic People of the Universe were arrested, tried, and convicted for aggravated hooliganism. Though the Plastics were far outside Havel's social and intellectual circles, he dived into a defense of the band, arguing, "If today young people with long hair are condemned for their unconventional music as criminals without notice, it will be all that much easier tomorrow to condemn in the same way other artists for their novels, poems, essays, and paintings."

Many other writers and artists signed on to Havel's letter, arguing that a threat to expression somewhere was a threat to speech everywhere. But Havel's reaction to the trial was both deeper and more nuanced. It was both personal and metaphoric:

> It does not happen often and usually it happens at moments when few expect it: something somewhere snaps and an event—thanks to an unpredictable synergy of its own internal prerequisites and of more or less random external circumstances—suddenly oversteps the limits of its position in the context of habitual everydayness, breaks the crust of what it is supposed to be and what it appears to be, and suddenly discloses its innermost, hidden and in some respects, symbolic meaning.

From that point on, Havel was on a collision course with Czech authorities, resulting in several arrests and prison stays, the longest extending from 1979 until 1983. As Zantovsky characterizes it, rarely has a political movement been born requiring "nothing more and nothing less than staying true to oneself."

In the ongoing argument among American writers and artists about whether we have an obligation to participate in public life, I fall firmly in the "yes" camp. I am afraid, though, up to now my reasons have been pretty vague—or, to put a more positive spin on it—mostly intuitive. But Zantovsky gives us an up-close look at what it really means for a writer to be at the center of a revolution. There is, of course, what Zantovsky calls the "strangely bookish tinge to modern Czech history," but he also offers us a deeply personal portrait of a man who was all artist and yet was so engaged in the fate of his country that he became the face of a revolution and its first postcommunist president.

Václav Havel brought the interiority and relentless self-examination of his plays to his life as both dissident and president. As Zantovsky puts it, "Havel offered his own criterion of an artist's value, a criterion he did his best to live up to for the rest of his life. It was to live a 'spiritual story.'" Havel's interiority was not rooted in the stereotype of the tortured artist or even in mere disposition; it was at the heart of Havel's beef with the communists. In one of the high points of the book, Zantovsky recalls the speech that President Havel gave to a joint meeting of the U.S. Congress in February 1990. Havel brought the legislators to their feet when he said, "The salvation of this human world lies nowhere else than in the human heart, in the human power to reflect, in human meekness and in human responsibility." Even so, several members asked Havel afterward what he had meant when he said, "Consciousness precedes being and not the other way around."

That last statement encapsulates Havel's central dispute with the architects of central European communism. One hundred fifty years earlier, Karl Marx had written, "Consciousness does not determine life, but life determines consciousness." Marx believed that the self is constructed by a person's position in the society, particularly by his or her economic position. Stalin took it one step further when he famously toasted members of the Writers' Union: "The production of souls is more important than the production of tanks. . . . And therefore I raise my glass to you, writers, the engineers of the human soul."

Havel as writer and activist and president never strayed from a central faith that human consciousness is inherent to the individual. He believed that the essential self is vulnerable to the influence of authoritarianism and crass consumerism, but it is also the key to liberty. In his most widely read and distributed essay, "The Power of the Powerless," Havel argues that each individual has the ability to resist and ultimately topple authoritarianism by withholding what he calls "ritual approval" from an ideological regime. As Zantovsky summarizes it, "The human capacity to live in truth to reaffirm man's authentic identity is the nuclear weapon that gives power to the powerless."

The example Havel uses is a greengrocer who dutifully displays a window placard provided by the authorities that says, "Workers of the world, unite!" Everyone knows that the placard is unlikely to reflect the greengrocer's own feelings or ideas, nor is it a genuine attempt to persuade passersby of anything in particular. Rather, it is a signal of compliance with the regime. As Havel puts it, "I am obedient and therefore I have the right to be left in peace."

But Havel imagines another future for the greengrocer.

What if the greengrocer "snaps" and stops putting out the sign? Yes, Havel knows that the greengrocer will be punished by the authorities, that the "anonymous components of the system will spew the greengrocer from its mouth." But he also imagines a more exalted role for him. By refusing to post a sign that is meaningless to him, the greengrocer upends the compliance on which the totalitarian system depends. He destabilizes everything. Havel writes:

> The singular, explosive, incalculable political power of living within the truth resides in the fact that living openly within the truth has an ally, invisible to be sure, but omnipresent: this hidden sphere. It is from this sphere that life lived openly in the truth grows; it is to this sphere that it speaks, and in it that it finds understanding. This is where the potential for communication exists. But this place is hidden and therefore, from the perspective of power, very dangerous.

Here we encounter something of a miracle: an actual politician who staked his very existence on the primacy and power of the inner life. In the period since the remarkable events of 1989, we have told ourselves reams of stories about the vanquishing of communism and Havel's role in making it happen. The dominant—almost unquestioned—story is one of unregulated and vibrant free-market capitalism freeing the people from their bleak lives under communism. We tell ourselves that the communitarian spirit at the heart of communist doctrine proved to be a fallacy and that the new manifest destiny, that of a worldwide consumer-driven market, celebrated a happy victory, a classic tale of good over evil.

But Havel's story—and his struggle with the communists in power in Czechoslovakia—simply had nothing to do with the market or the free flow of consumer goods. Havel's struggle was not economic; it was intellectual and emotional and spiritual. It was humanistic. This was not the stuff of grand powers competing, but a worldview specifically grounded in the importance of elevating and protecting the individual consciousness and its yearning to flourish in the open.

Just writing this presses on a deep bruise. It feels something like homesickness or nostalgia or regret. Some of it has to do with a yearning for the irresistible mix of art, wine-soaked parties, and revolutionary thinking. And—in the spirit of true confession—I was actually in Czechoslovakia and Hungary and Poland (and the USSR and East Germany and Yugoslavia, for that matter) during the fall and winter of 1989, but I was a brand-new college graduate, a backpacker so far out of the action that I didn't have a real sense of the import of what was brewing until the Berlin Wall was actually breached. In fact, as I read Zantovsky's book, I felt a little sheepish that I didn't take better notes about the world-changing events transpiring around me.

Even so, the overwhelming feeling I nursed throughout the book was not nostalgia for that particular trip or time, but a kind of longing for the purpose and community that Havel and his "bag of fleas"—as both friends and detractors called his inner circle of writers, artists, and intellectuals—brought to the Velvet Revolution. It is similar to the feeling I get when I fantasize about being a nun on the bus—riding with my friends, fighting for justice, and whispering "Screw you" to House Speaker Ryan and Pope Benedict XVI. It's the feeling I had when I visited

Reykjavik earlier this summer. There I had coffee with the MP and self-proclaimed "poetician" Birgitta Jónsdóttir. I had been following her work since she was part of the movement that brought down the government and a lot of reckless bankers following the 2008 financial crisis. But when we walked into the beautiful terrace coffee shop above the bookstore, we bumped into a performance artist who had run for president, a painter who had found his life's work when he lost his job in the financial crash, a cofounder of Iceland's Pirate Party, and a mishmash of other artists and activists the likes of which I never run across in my neighborhood coffee shop.

The more I examine these feelings, the more I believe they are not just symptoms of a romantic temperament. They are rooted in longings that should be attended to. I wonder if nostalgia for Velvet Revolutionary Czechoslovakia does not belong to me alone. I wonder if it isn't symptomatic of a kind of collective homesickness for our own inner lives and for genuine connection to one another. I wonder if it isn't grounded in a deep alienation generated by the enormous institutions—private and public alike—that seem both omnipotent and omniscient.

One of the reasons I think this isn't just me is that, a few years ago, I had the chance to work on back-to-back projects— one that brought me in close contact with activists in the Tea Party uprising and another that allowed me to get to know members of the Occupy movement. Though they agitated in separate spheres, the heart of their fears and dissatisfactions were remarkably similar. Both groups felt acted on and dehumanized by huge, impersonal institutions. Tea Party members pinned their grievances on big government; Occupy activists targeted huge financial institutions. And all this in addition to blanket government surveillance, relentless police brutality, and a massive system protecting the haves and distracting the have-nots. It's no wonder, then, that we might feel a little kinship with Czechs living behind the Iron Curtain.

But Havel was clear in where he placed both responsibility and hope. Unlike Samuel Beckett and some of his other artistic contemporaries, Havel believed that existential loneliness is not intrinsic to the human condition but is the consequence of "desocializing properties of the governing system."

That analysis has some resonance for our moment in time and place in the world. Americans have less trust in institutions than ever before, and increasing numbers are beginning to question the hegemony created by concentrated money and power. I recently met a woman at a public library program (and though I can't say for sure, I suspect her place on the political spectrum is a long way from mine) who said, "You know it is in their"—and by "they" she meant corporate and government—"interests to keep us away from one another because if we were to meet, we might like each other and agree that we're all getting screwed."

This is right-over-the-plate Havelian thinking, and we would be well served to take another look at what he has to offer. As he put it in "The Power of the Powerless":

> A person who has been seduced by the consumer value system, whose identity is dissolved in an amalgam of the accoutrements of mass civilization, and who has no roots in the order of being, no sense of responsibility for anything higher than his own personal survival, is a demoralized person. The system depends on this demoralization, deepens it, is in fact a projection of it into society. Living within the

truth, as humanity's revolt against an enforced position, is, on the contrary, an attempt to regain control over one's own sense of responsibility.

Maybe that is what I'm homesick for. Maybe that is what the woman in the library and the Tea Partiers and the Occupy diehards were talking about. Maybe we are all longing for the chance to take responsibility for our own lives and our own communities. Maybe we are looking to find a space in which our own idiosyncratic thoughts and dreams are respected and treated as worthy of consideration. And maybe we are looking for a place to build a movement—a society—based on moral choice and shared responsibility. And if Havel is a patron saint for our time, maybe that's not a bad basis for a revolution.

This line of thinking requires a warning label, however. As Havel put it in "The Power of the Powerless," "it is an all-or-nothing gamble" to dig deep into our innermost selves and hold ourselves and one another accountable for "living in truth." And holding oneself to that standard while trying to live a public life is crushing. Governing was an excruciating business for Václav Havel. Nearly half the time he was in office, he was suffering or recovering from a serious illness. He endured nasty personal criticism, humiliation in the press, and the breakup of a country. And yet, amid all of that, he continued to examine his own inner motives through an exacting moral lens. While he was president, he wrote, "I am constantly preparing for the last judgement, for the highest court from which nothing can be hidden, which will appreciate everything that should be appreciated, and which will, of course, notice anything that is not in its place."

All this is to say that it is a steep and jagged road to take responsibility for ourselves and our own liberty. Let's return to our plucky greengrocer. He refused to put out his sign, risking economic ruin and arrest. What about us? No one is requiring us to sport bumper stickers declaring "Surveillance: It's Everywhere You Want to Be" or "I ♥ Unregulated Free-Market Capitalism."

But as with the citizens of Havel's Czechoslovakia, the systems that create our malaise are at least somewhat dependent on our participation and compliance. Edward Snowden told us that the U.S. government—in cahoots with the corporate masters of the internet—is gathering massive quantities of personal data on American citizens. We tell ourselves that we are willing to trade a bit of privacy for increased security. But in reality, it is convenience, not security, that swamps our ability to protect personal privacy and autonomy. Nothing beats the convenience of our online lives—sitting on the couch in our sweatpants, banking and grocery shopping and stalking our exes all while keeping up with MLB box scores. We can gas up our cars on any street corner and find the brand of cereal we want in any store in America and never have to be too hot or too cold or even wait very long for anything. But we—and by "we," I mean relatively affluent twenty-first-century Americans—are living in a Potemkin village. Flawless convenience and near-perfect comfort cannot protect us from our status as mammals and mortals. They cannot protect us from disaster or loss or death. Convenience on demand can't protect us from—and in fact is escalating—an unhealthy ecosystem, economic injustice, and a runaway climate crisis. Ultimately, our discomfort with discomfort makes us less able to cope with the human condition—both politically and personally.

So while Havel's greengrocer was called to truth in the face of ideological totalitarianism, we are called to the truth of our own participation in an economic and political system that reinforces power disparities, income inequality, and ecological recklessness. If the greengrocer chooses to live in truth, he risks arrest, placing him alongside activists from across the globe, including those in our own country, who risk everything. As for me and others like me, though, if we choose to live in truth, we risk inconvenience, aggravation, and discomfort.

I don't say any of this to minimize the cost of the call. It is a call that requires us to be steady and mature against ubiquitous modeling to the contrary. It requires an inner eye that is unwavering in the face of the seductive temptation to look the other way. It subjects us to mocking and ridicule. And because we are human, any attempt to live in truth means we will certainly fail. We will come face-to-face with our own complicities and shortcomings. We will have to say "I don't know" and "I am sorry" and "Maybe you're right." We will have to say "I was shallow and untrustworthy." We will have to say "This time I failed." We will have to ask genuine questions and sit in restless discomfort and admit our own weaknesses. In the end, we will have to risk what Havel risked. Everything. We will have to risk ruin.

September 2015

The Word Made Flesh

On Encountering the Work of Marcel Broodthaers

> *And the Word was made flesh, and dwelt*
> *among us, and we beheld his glory, the glory*
> *as of the only begotten of the Father, full of*
> *grace and truth.*
>
> —John 1:14

I HAVE AN ODDLY RITUALIZED RELATIONSHIP WITH NEW York City. It is probably because deep down I suspect I missed something essential by never having lived there. I had a close call in my early twenties, then reversed course and moved to Washington, D.C. From my faraway perch here in the Pacific Northwest, New York has always seemed to be where real things happen before they ricochet off in some diminished form to the rest of the country. But I go once or twice a year to nurse my regrets and feed my cultural appetites. There are a few things I do every time, rain or shine, summer or winter. I walk around the reservoir in Central Park. I browse the Strand. And I go to MoMA. My rituals and habits help me feel like I belong, like I somehow know New York in the way that well-trodden paths create a kind of bodily knowing.

On a recent visit, in true ritualist fashion, I dragged my husband up Fifth Avenue to MoMA. I had been there earlier in the winter to see a Picasso retrospective and had bumped into a small but mighty Pollock exhibition that culminates in a few of the huge numbered paintings he made at the height of his career. David is a heart-and-soul devotee of Jackson Pollock, so I knew I could lure him up there without too much cajoling. As for me, I was going just because that's what I do. We slowly picked through the Pollock show, dizzying and glum as it is, and then headed upstairs to the special exhibit, which we knew nothing about.

The exhibit turned out to be the first New York retrospective of the work of Marcel Broodthaers, a Belgian poet turned visual artist, who died in 1976 at the age of fifty-two. We often fantasize about what we will do when we abandon poetry. David says cobbler. I choose seamstress. Or pie maker. Anything to avoid the existential aggravation that comes from tying yourself in knots for a readership that seems to be made up almost exclusively of other poets. So Broodthaers was appealing from the get-go.

Broodthaers is most often characterized as a conceptualist swimming with the likes of Magritte and Duchamp. And indeed, he is probably most famous for his *Museum of Modern Art, Department of Eagles*, which excels in irony and is brimming with concept. *Museum of Modern Art*—in which Broodthaers declared he was no longer an artist but a museum curator—debuted in his Brussels home in 1968, and parts of it appeared in various European cities until 1971, when he proclaimed the museum bankrupt and announced that he was once again an artist. Not quite the Artist Formerly Known as Prince kind of stuff, but a close cousin.

In a move that now looks like a pattern, Broodthaers first announced his abandonment of poetry and embrace of the visual arts in 1964, after having spent several months holed up in his new studio. In the catalog for his first show, he wrote, "I, too, wondered whether I could not sell something and succeed in life. For some time, I have been no good at anything. Finally the idea of inventing something insincere crossed my mind and I set to work straightaway."

In that first show, Broodthaers encased leftover copies of his book of poems, *Pense-Bête*, in plaster, eggshells, and plastic balls. The overall effect is both desecratory and dear. While it clearly could be interpreted as a rejection of poetry—something like "I am done with this art and all its petty, ephemeral preoccupations, I therefore subsume it into the more substantial, ocular, high-flying conceptual world"—it also has a quality of grasping for solidity and permanence, as if the paper and the sentiment that make up these poems are too fragile to hold up to the forces of the world without a little plaster to stabilize them.

Though I identify strongly with the impulse behind *Pense-Bête*, I am most attracted to the work that immediately follows it. Broodthaers spent from 1964 to 1968 building large sculptural pieces featuring shellacked mussel shells and heaps of cracked eggshells.

Because of the tinted shellac, the mussel shells have a slick blue sheen, and they are packed into pieces like *Cercle de moules*, a probably four-by-four mounted circle of nothing but mussel shells and the overflowing mussel pot of *Triomphe de moule I*. In the exhibit, the blue-black of the mussels is balanced by the contrasting use of eggshells in separate but complementary pieces. Allegedly, Broodthaers got the shells from Brussels restaurants after they were cracked and discarded. He attached eggshells to a painted Belgian flag; he stuffed a hutch painted eggshell-white with more eggshells. There is white canvas dotted with eggs, and there is a stool also covered in eggs.

The shells (both egg and mussel) are alluring in their own way, and are strangely homey. They have a kind of sweetness and humbleness to them, and there is something moving about their creatureness being preserved all this time, rescued from restaurant trash fifty years ago.

Granted, I am susceptible to the pretty, and these pieces are very pretty in their monochromatic simplicity and fragility. I cannot stop thinking about how hard it must be to transport these pieces across the Atlantic without a catastrophe of shattering shells.

Though Broodthaers had no way to know it, his shell pieces speak directly to the longings of this moment. Twenty-first-century life is so theoretical, so arm's length. So digitized and ethereal and relentless. I can watch elephants in their native habitat one second, then try to find the name of the neighbors' roses that are yellow in the middle and red on the outside (answer: Rainbow Sunblaze floribunda). Then I can diagnose why I have a rash on my wrist and check whether my daughter has turned in her math homework and communally speculate about who last saw Prince alive. I can even find links to breathtaking poems I would never have otherwise read. I can also feed, or at least try to feed, some of the basest needs of my reptile brain— connection, approval, a dopamine hit from someone who announces they like my latest poem, my haircut, my daughter's haircut, my dog's haircut.

Anxiety slinks close behind. If approval traffic is slow, I wonder what is wrong with my poem, my pithy observation, my haircut. And while we are out seeking assurance we are liked and admired, we are barraged by the stacked lunacy of presidential primaries, police brutality, genocide, drone strikes, ISIS, Islamophobia, Zika virus, flash floods, suicide bombers, child pornographers, bike accidents, cancer scares, the ailments of aging parents, teenage angst, and amped-up homeland security. It's all there and not there at the same time.

I recently heard the Zen saying "No matter how many times you say the word 'water,' it will never be wet." It's an exhortation toward direct experience, though when I first heard it, I resisted its tone of wise certainty. I do believe in the power of words. I believe in the power of words to make me feel wet even as my skin and hair remain dry. But despite my career as a stubborn evangelist of the word, I am moved by the directness of Broodthaers's eggs and mussels. They transport me to another family's breakfast table. Into the life of a single office worker stopping for *moules-frites* on his way home to his dim apartment. They reek with sorrow for the chickens and the mussels, too. What about the busboy who cleared the plates? And who separated the trash?

There is one piece in particular that reveals the shallowness of Broodthaers's bravado. He said he did it for the money, the art, but *Maria* is where his tenderness leaks through. *Maria* is simple enough—a navy-blue housedress hung on a wooden hanger with the belt draped from it as it would be in the closet. Tied to the bottom of the right sleeve is a paper shopping sack printed with a faded cheese ad and dotted with broken eggshells. As these things do, the dress seems impossibly small and frail. But the cracked, stained, and haphazard eggshells glued to the shopping bag are all dailiness and loss and brokenness. It's as if mortality attached itself to a paper sack.

It makes me feel naïve and provincial to respond to a major New York retrospective in such a simplistic emotional way. And in ordinary times, I would have walked away with a vague sense of affection for Broodthaers and his rollicking and tender transition from poet to conceptualist. I would have felt sad about his early death. But on March 21, 2016—two days after we visited MoMA—three men blew themselves up in massive, coordinated bombings in Brussels. Two were in the airport. One was at a Metro station. Thirty-two people were killed, and over three hundred were injured. The news of the attacks spurred another worldwide wave of fear and recrimination, knocking even the circus created by then-candidate Donald Trump out of the headlines for a day or two.

Though I hate to admit such superficiality, the experience of having been to the Broodthaers exhibit made Belgium feel much closer. Not only could I envision Brussels more clearly, but it sharpened my physical connection to the event itself. I could almost feel the reverberations of the blasts tremor through my body.

In the ensuing—and righteous—debate over why we publicly mourn brutal attacks in Brussels and Paris more than we do the ones in Lahore and Iskandariya and Kabul, we are right to question whether we are racist and colonialist and Eurocentric in valuing some lives over others. But I wonder if some of our failures in attention also stem from a lack of experience and from a lack of imagination. In the same way that I have created a goat path from our Midtown hotel up to MoMA in order to reaffirm my connection to New York City, the Broodthaers exhibit gave me a bodily connection to Brussels that I would not have had without it. It was as if he gave me a spark of connection to what for me was an otherwise theoretical place.

That is not to say that we should not interrogate our own callousness toward brutality everywhere, particularly if it is informed by colonialism and racism, but it is to affirm the value of art like that of the Broodthaers shell period. The straightforward connection to the body created by pieces like *Maria* tied me to Belgium physically and viscerally, increasing my imagination in favor of the people of Brussels.

That is a feat in this era of twenty-four-hour breaking news, maudlin public mourning, and compassion fatigue. Broodthaers delivers breakfasts and dinners and offbeat patriotism. He forces me to imagine chickens and dockworkers and dishwashers with their particular sufferings and quickly passing lives. His work expands who I worry about and who I mourn. It takes Belgium off the map and places it squarely in the kitchen. It makes metaphor three-dimensional. It gives poetry flesh.

January 2017

These Are Strange
Times, My Dear

Considering Ai Weiwei's @Large

I HAVE BEEN IN A LOT OF PRISONS. IN NEARLY TEN YEARS
as a public defender, I visited federal prisons and state mental
hospitals and county jails. I visited maximum security peniten-
tiaries and halfway houses and work camps. I don't have any romantic notions—or even much residual curiosity—about what
happens behind bars. But when I learned about *@Large*, the installation art exhibit at Alcatraz created by superstar Chinese
artist Ai Weiwei and the For-Site Foundation, I immediately
bought tickets for myself and my husband. I was eager to see Ai
Weiwei's work in person, and the description of the show tapped
into my fears about increasing repression of dissent and threats
to free speech in the United States and around the world:

@Large turns Alcatraz into a space for dialogue about how we define liberty and justice, individual rights and personal responsibility. In artworks that balance political impact with aesthetic grace, the exhibition directly and imaginatively addresses the situation of people around the world who have been deprived of their freedom for speaking out about their beliefs—people like Ai himself.

During the early March weekend we visited, cool mornings were followed by warm and sunny afternoons. As we flew from the north over the estuary and the newly green spring hills, it was hard not to wonder why everyone doesn't live—or want to live—in San Francisco. The combination of water and sun, charming architecture, polite and health-conscious residents, and tidy streets all add up to an unpunctured nimbus of well-being. It seems as if San Francisco has it all figured out, as if there must be less suffering there. It's as if all that inconspicuous but ubiquitous wealth has rubbed the jagged edges off urban life and scrubbed the wind of late-winter cold.

We stayed at Union Square, easy walking distance from some of the city's famously beautiful neighborhoods, including Chinatown, which promised to be good fun that weekend of the Chinese New Year Parade, which—according to the hotel's smilingly helpful valet—is one of the ten best parades in the world.

And yet, incongruously, one of San Francisco's most popular destinations is the remains of a brutal and notorious prison. The bouncy yellow light and temperate Pacific breezes don't exactly suggest hard labor and isolation, but from 1934 to 1963 Alcatraz was a dreadful and dreaded place. It housed some of the nation's most infamous and violent criminals, including Al Capone and the "Birdman of Alcatraz," Robert Stroud. In the early years, there was a rule of silence banning almost all talking that drove many of the prisoners nearly mad. In the end, Capone was reported to have said, "It looks like Alcatraz has got me licked."

Alcatraz also was the site of one of the most well-known and successful Native rights protests in American history. In 1969—after the prison had closed—American Indian Movement (AIM) activists took over and occupied Alcatraz, which helped instigate a number of federal reforms, including the official end of tribal terminations. The occupation came to tragic conclusion when a child fell from a third-floor window and the remaining protesters were removed from the property. Now Alcatraz is a national park and bird refuge, hosting 1.5 million visitors every year.

On the day we were scheduled to visit the island, we set out on foot toward the ferry terminal. We walked through the gassy dome of the Stockton Street Tunnel and were dumped directly into the heart of a bustling Chinatown. It was barely 9:00 a.m., and while the neighborhood around Union Square was sparsely populated with joggers and small groups of sunglasses-clad tourists carrying paper coffee cups, Chinatown was going at full tilt. Stockton Street was packed with people—mostly speaking Chinese—walking in and out of greengrocers, chatting on the sidewalks, and hurrying from one place to another. The neon signs were all in Chinese, and—on the second and third floors—windows were flung open to reveal wire hangers draped with shirts and socks and underthings pushed out into the sun to dry. The sidewalks were lined with bins of dried shrimp and ginseng and rice, and the shops were overflowing with the gorgeous fruits and vegetables of Northern California. There were heads of cabbage and bok choy and huge globe grapes. There were snake beans and broccoli spears and dusty mauve eggplants. And there were also things I couldn't identify—jagged red tubers that looked like artichokes but weren't, a bright green vegetable that resembled an oversized and wrinkled cucumber, and an alluring rosy fruit that suggested "mango" but was not quite.

We jostled our way through the streets, mumbling "Excuse me" and taking care not to splash coffee on those we bumped up against. But then, as soon as we crossed the street into North Beach, the sidewalks became sleepy and abandoned again. It was as if we had passed through a bright dream of China on our way to visit one of its most famous dissident sons.

Once we arrived at Pier 33—where the Alcatraz ferry takes off—there was no mistaking it for anywhere but the America of capitalism and spectacle. The wharf was crawling with strollers and down vests and breakfast burritos. We plodded alongside other bleary tourists as we carried our preprinted boarding passes through stanchioned switchbacks. A man in a sharp green polo shirt took our tickets, smiled mellowly, and said, "Have a great time." Right before we boarded the ferry, we passed through a staging area where a commercial photographer was taking pictures of slightly dazed families posing in front of a huge plastic photograph of Alcatraz. "No, thanks," David quipped as we passed by the photographer. "We don't need to give the NSA a snapshot."

Most everybody around us was talking about the weather and restaurants and plans for the rest of the weekend. They were decidedly not talking about why they were going to Alcatraz, what they thought about the work of Ai Weiwei, or how they felt about the government spying program recently revealed by Edward Snowden. And nobody around us was talking about mass incarceration or political repression, either.

I had recently read that only 40 percent of Americans opposed the U.S. program of widespread, suspicionless surveillance. That was consistent with my friends' and students' attitudes. As one of them put it, "I'm not doing anything wrong, so I don't care." On a Saturday morning in a line full of strangers, I couldn't pull myself out of my natural reticence to ask their thoughts on these matters, as much as I was desperate to know. So—ironically—I settled for eavesdropping.

Though you wouldn't detect it from the carnival atmosphere on Pier 33, these are unnerving times. There is a kind of capricious depravity at large that has us looking over our shoulders and wringing our hands. Each time we turn on our televisions or computers, there is ISIS, speaking the Queen's English and beheading people in highly produced infomercials. There are radicals slaughtering cartoonists at their desks and others dragging schoolgirls into the forest. There are unhinged gunmen shooting American students at a dizzying rate. And airline pilots flying planes into mountains and downing others into the sea, not to mention the countless acts of daily violence and cruelty being carried out in our homes and neighborhoods.

Meanwhile, those who are commissioned to protect us are enacting their own brutalities. Last year, we read with horror the Senate Intelligence Committee's report that implicated the CIA in using sleep deprivation, waterboarding, and rectal feeding during interrogations, while in the first five months of 2015, 385

Americans—most of them young men of color—were shot and killed by the police in their own communities. Last summer, we watched night after night as demonstrators in Ferguson, Missouri, protested the shooting of an unarmed black teenager by a white police officer. And in addition to the arrest of hundreds of protesters, journalists covering the demonstrations were also threatened, harassed, and arrested by militarized riot police.

According to PEN International, in the first half of 2014 alone, 810 writers and journalists were arrested, detained, or killed by authorities around the world. And almost daily we learn about the ever-more-sophisticated and intrusive ways that governments monitor and record the activities of the world's citizens. As playwright Tom Stoppard recently wrote in the *Guardian*, "The world of surveillance operated by the people we pay to guard us exceeds the fevered dreams of the Stasi."

I first started paying attention to Ai Weiwei in 2010 when he filled the enormous Turbine Hall of the Tate Modern in London with a hundred million individually cast and painted porcelain sunflower seeds. The sunflower seeds were made in Jingdezhen, a city that has been celebrated for its porcelain for seventeen hundred years. Sixteen hundred people worked on the project, and each seed went through a thirty-step process before it was painted and fired at thirteen hundred degrees and then poured, with the rest of the hundred million seeds, onto the concrete floor of the hall. I couldn't help but hear the echo of the famous Allen Ginsberg poem "Sunflower Sutra":

> —We're not our skin of grime, we're not dread bleak dusty imageless locomotives, we're golden sunflowers inside, blessed by our own seed & hairy naked accomplishment-bodies

growing into mad black formal sunflowers in the sunset, spied on by our own eyes under the shadow of the mad loco-motive riverbank sunset Frisco hilly tincan evening sitdown vision.

There must be something about a sunflower, because Ai Weiwei's 2010 exhibit also asserted a vision of shimmering indi-viduals in the face of a bleak consumerist and repressive culture. As Ai put it: "Seeds grow.... The crowd will have its way, even-tually." Though the metaphor offered by *Sunflower Seeds* was not particularly subtle—Ai himself said he wants "people who don't understand art to understand what I am doing"—it made the point without reverting to the dissonance or incoherence that often marks conceptualist installations. In fact, in their tiny, precise detail, the seeds themselves were almost sweet.

It turns out that the combination of sweet and unsubtle is Ai Weiwei's signature stance. In November 2013, he tweeted his intention to place a fresh bouquet of flowers in the front basket of a bicycle parked outside his Beijing studio every morning until his passport is returned by the government. His passport was confiscated in April 2011, and Ai has been unable to leave China since. His floral resistance has generated the #flowersforfreedom hashtag under which people from around the word tweet photo-graphs of flowers in protest of Ai's travel restrictions.

Despite the quietness of that protest, Ai's life has been marked with hardship from the beginning. Though his father— Ai Qing—was a widely read and mostly nonpolitical poet, he ran afoul of Mao Zedong and was branded a "rightist" following a brief period of free expression (called the Hundred Flowers Campaign, ironically). In 1958, when Ai Weiwei was only a year old, Ai Qing and his family were detained in a labor camp for dissidents. Later, during the Cultural Revolution, the family was sent to "little Siberia," where they lived in an underground cavern and Ai Qing was forced to clean the village's communal toilets.

Ai Weiwei moved to New York to study art in the early 1980s, where he befriended Allen Ginsberg and became acquainted with the art of Marcel Duchamp and other conceptualists whose work influences him to this day. Ai returned to China in 1993 to care for his ailing father and became internationally famous for, among other things, his design work on the Bird's Nest Stadium, which was the icon of the 2008 Beijing Olympics. But as he became increasingly critical of the government and more visible in China and abroad, he also became a target for the communist authorities. In 2009, he had emergency brain surgery following a police beating, and in 2010, the government demolished his newly built studio, claiming that it didn't have the necessary permits.

Then—on April 3, 2011—Ai Weiwei was removed from a flight bound for Hong Kong and detained for eighty-one days, while artists and activists around the world protested his arrest and demanded to know where he had been taken. As he described later in the *Guardian*:

> During my detention in China I was watched 24 hours a day. The light was always on. There were two guards on two-hour shifts standing next to me—even watching when I swallowed a pill; I had to open my mouth so they could see my throat. You have to take a shower in front of them; they watch you while you brush your teeth, in the name of making

sure you're not hurting yourself. They had three surveillance cameras to make sure the guards would not communicate with me.

After nearly three months, Ai was released, charged with tax evasion, and stripped of his passport. Despite almost constant surveillance and travel restrictions since then, Ai continues to criticize the Chinese government and to participate in installations in China and abroad. Despite the fact that Ai Weiwei was unable to visit Alcatraz, he eagerly joined the partnership with the For-Site Foundation, which offered him the opportunity to shape an exhibit there. He designed the installation based on photographs, stories, drawings, and maps of the prison; and he monitored closely the execution of his vision. Some of the artists and volunteers who installed the exhibition wore GoPro cameras attached to their heads so that Ai could supervise the process from his studio in China.

Dock to dock, the ferry ride to Alcatraz takes fifteen minutes, so much of the actual boat time is consumed with loading, safety briefings, and instructions for disembarking. A few minutes from mooring, a short prerecorded audio presentation blasted over the loudspeakers, briefing sightseers about Alcatraz's history as a federal prison, then as the site of the AIM protest, and now as a national park and bird refuge. After again wishing us a good day, the audio wrapped up: "Alcatraz. It's so much more than just a prison." I laughed aloud and looked around to share the joke, but no one else seemed to have been listening. Mostly, they were taking pictures of one another and themselves in front of the looming island and its ruins.

In the midst of all the high spirits and flawless helpfulness, I spotted a large sign above the dock that read, "Your cell is subject to search at any time. Contraband items found in your cell will be confiscated and a disciplinary report will be placed against you for possession of same." I immediately turned to David and mouthed, "What the hell?" and then, just as quickly, realized that the sign was a replica of one that had hung at Alcatraz when it was still a prison. For a split second, I had actually believed that the National Park Service was reserving the right to search our cell phones.

As soon as the ferry docked—even before we began to unload—a barrel-chested ranger wearing a Smokey Bear hat began welcoming us to Alcatraz over the shore PA system. He bantered with folks as they got off the boat, taking wagers on who had come from farthest away and pointing out the nearest restrooms, which he called "the loo." Once we were all gathered around him on the plaza, he asked people to raise their hands if they were there to see the Ai Weiwei exhibit. About a quarter of us raised our hands, and he pointed us up the hill to the New Industries Building, shooing us away with yet another "Have a good time" and a reminder not to eat or drink anywhere except on the dock.

The entrance to the Ai exhibit was, not surprisingly, dramatic. The front door of the New Industries Building—which had been the laundry and mending shop for the prison (making me wonder about what made those industries "new" and reminding me of the Robert Hass poem: "All the new thinking is about loss. / In this it resembles all the old thinking")—was filled with the head of a huge paper-and-bamboo dragon. Its crayon-box colors, curled whiskers, and goggly eyes all signaled friendliness in the vein of Toothless from *How to Train Your Dragon* rather than fierceness à la Smaug of *The Hobbit*. I realized later that the pupils that gave the dragon's eyes their goggliness were replicas of the Twitter logo, Ai Weiwei's favorite means of communication, despite that it's banned in China.

Behind the enormous head—which was shipped to San Francisco suspended in a gigantic crate—wound a body and a tail that was at least a hundred yards long, consisting of rainbow-colored circles joined by bamboo rods. Many of the circles were painted with bright scales and flowers, but they were intermittently punctuated with circles featuring quotes from individuals from around the globe who have been detained or harassed by their governments, including Edward Snowden and Nelson Mandela, Le Quoc Quan, and Irom Sharmila Chanu. A quote from Ai Weiwei himself—"Every one of us is a potential convict"—pierced the voyeuristic remove of tourists visiting Alcatraz between a morning walk across the Golden Gate Bridge and an evening game at AT&T Park.

But voyeurism is the stock-in-trade of Alcatraz, and nothing cuts across cultures like the titillating promise of a notorious prison. Despite at least a half-day commitment and a thirty-dollar ticket price, five thousand people a day visit Alcatraz, and the organizers anticipate that five hundred thousand of them will see at least part of the Ai Weiwei exhibit during its run. On the day we visited, the crowd was more heterogeneous than the audience of any other art exhibit I've ever attended. There were folks of many races, cultures, and—presumably—creeds, small children and senior citizens, gay couples and straight couples, mothers and daughters. People came right up to the dragon, causing it to tremble on its wires. As I watched a family with three young children come within inches of the fragile whiskers and snout, I said to the docent I had been chatting with: "That must be nerve-wracking. Those whiskers look like they could break off in a second."

"Oh, it is," she replied. "But that's how he wants it."

"Ai Weiwei?"

"Yes. He wants the dragon to have a chance to move, even if it is caused by the breath and steps of people walking by."

I thought back on that conversation later that evening as we watched the dragon dances in the Chinese New Year's Parade—block after block of dancers running through the streets at full speed, lifting the dragons high above their heads and menacing children and tourists as the dragons chased after the lead dancers, who were bearing volleyball-sized pearls on the end of long sticks. The firecrackers and screeching toddlers and spotlights and drums made me think back to Ai Weiwei's bright dragon, which must have been—by that time of night—utterly still in the dark laundry on Alcatraz.

It reminded me a bit of the days when I had just begun to work as a public defender. As I was out living my life—going to concerts, hanging out with friends—I would randomly burst into tears, overcome by the fact that a client whom I had seen earlier in the day was sitting alone in his cell for the night. Or at least that's what I imagined he was doing. The daily pleasures of my life brought home the realities of incarceration. Though I often spent hours a day in some form of lockup, I could always leave, while my clients usually couldn't. And in San Francisco, I could spend the time and money to be reminded of those who are detained by repressive governments, but then I could move on to an overpriced dinner and a raucous parade while the "With

Wind" dragon and the people it called attention to remained in their dim cells.

The second large room in the New Industries Building was filled with "Trace," a massive, brightly colored Lego installation composed of 176 portraits of artists, writers, and activists who have been imprisoned or otherwise persecuted by their governments. According to another friendly art student on duty for the day, the panels were built from 1.2 million Lego bricks and were assembled by eighty volunteers in accordance with Ai Weiwei's designs. The portraits were laid out in five large panels spreading across the peeling concrete floor and covering at least another eighty yards of the laundry. The portraits were varying sizes and colors, with different typefaces identifying each person depicted, including Nelson Mandela and Ta Phong Tan, Eskinder Nega and Lolo, and Gedhun Choeky Nyima, the six-year-old who was abducted by the Chinese government after he was named the Panchen Lama.

To me, the most striking part of "Trace" was the inclusion of Edward Snowden and Chelsea Manning. It was unsettling to see Snowden, who is still in limbo in Russia, and Manning, who is serving a thirty-five-year sentence in Leavenworth for providing classified documents to WikiLeaks, celebrated as free-speech martyrs right in front of a phalanx of rangers on the federal government payroll, most of them grinning and reminding us to "have a great time."

Later, in the cafeteria of the main prison, visitors were invited to write words of encouragement on postcards addressed to the writers and activists who were pictured in "Trace." The postcards were decorated with birds and plants from the countries where the prisoners were being held. I chose three postcards at random

and ended up selecting Jamaloddin Khanjani, who is serving
a twenty-year sentence for spreading propaganda against Iran;
Mohammed al-Ajami, who is serving a fifteen-year sentence for
writing and reading a poem critical of the emir in Qatar; and
Chelsea Manning. When I sat down to fill them out, all I could
think to write was "Keep the faith." I felt like I was writing a
note in an eighth-grade yearbook ("Stay foxy. Never change"),
and that faith might be the only thing that tied Mohammed al-
Ajami and Chelsea Manning and me together.

Despite the scale and flash of "With Wind" and "Trace,"
the most affecting parts of the exhibit—those that managed to
get beyond broad statements and primary colors—were those
that were the most interior, those that invited us to imagine the
experience of incarceration. In "Stay Tuned," Ai Weiwei and
his collaborators took over twelve tiny cells with cracked walls
and exposed plumbing, each lit by a single bulb, into which they
broadcast the work of artists and activists who had been imprisoned at some point. The works varied from Martin Luther
King Jr.'s "Beyond Vietnam" speech to "Virgin Mary, Put Putin
Away" by Pussy Riot to "Sorrow Tears and Blood" by Nigerian
musician and activist Fela Kuti. Visitors were invited to step inside the cells and sit on a single metal stool facing the wall to
listen to a snippet of song or poem or speech piped in through
a vent. While it was fun to hear Pussy Riot's defiance, listening
to Iranian poet Ahmad Shamlou read his poem "In This Dead-
End Street" was essential and haunting. It was read in Persian,
and though I did not understand the language, it was as if I
could hear the voice inside his head as he wrote in isolation. In
the English translation posted outside the cell, the poem begins
here:

In this dead-end street
they smell your breath
lest, God forbid,
you've said I love you.
They sniff at your heart—
These are strange times, my dear
—and they flog love
by the side of the road at the barrier.
Love must be hidden at home in the closet.
In this crooked dead-end street, twisted with cold
they fuel their bonfire
with poems and songs.
Danger! Don't dare think.
These are strange times, my dear.
The knock on the door in the night
is someone who's come to snuff out the light.

As much as I admired "Stay Tuned," the piece that moved me most was "Refraction," also housed in the New Industries Building. "Refraction" is a five-ton model of a wing made from repurposed solar panels and household pots and kettles, all salvaged from the Tibetan plateau. In order to see the sculpture at the center of "Refraction," visitors have to walk along the "lower gun gallery" where guards once watched over inmates at work in the laundry. I never got an entirely clear view of "Refraction" through the crooked angles of the narrow gun gallery and the cracked wired glass. In many ways, it was that strain to apprehend that made the best use of Alcatraz's symbol-rich space.

The exhibit notes made much of the fact that—similar to "With Wind"—"Refraction" is a flightless wing inside an impenetrable prison. For me, though, the thing that was most affecting about "Refraction" was that it was just glimpsed, that it was nearly out of sight. It might have been imagined. It might have been manufactured by longing. Yes, by the longing for flight, but also by the longing for the comforts of home. From one angle, you could catch a clear look at a dented red aluminum teakettle. It was so homey and out of place that it nearly brought me to my knees. That teakettle belonged to a mother, to a grandmother. It was the teakettle at the center of the daily rituals that make up a life. And seeing it there, suspended on the edge of a massive metal wing behind cracked and broken glass, made it feel taunting and hallucinatory, as it must have felt sometimes for the inmates to see laundry fluttering inside the windows of the New Industries Building, reminding them of other bright mornings where the windows were thrown open to dry socks and shirts in the warm air.

The other unsettling aspect of "Refraction" is that the narrow hallways of the gun gallery overlooked not only the concrete room that contained the sculpture itself but also the main work space of the New Industries Building, where hundreds of people were walking through "With Wind" and "Trace." People were so tender in their unguarded state, moving their lips as they read, pointing out quotes to their children, sending text messages and taking selfies in front of the dragon. The walk along the hallway created a kind of forced watching that put *@Large* visitors in the position of both guard and inmate, both surveyor and surveilled.

Though I found "Stay Tuned" and "Refraction" to be both moving and evocative of the space, *@Large* as a whole was a little haphazard and incoherent. Though the overall message was loud, it wasn't very clear. It was a scattershot protest of repression in some of its multiple forms. Maybe that just reflects our own ambivalence and confusion about the state of the world, or maybe it was the result of both the venue and the intended audience. Ai Weiwei had the opportunity to reach hundreds of thousands of people and a chance to impress upon casual visitors the widespread government practice of arrest and intimidation. Though it is hard to say whether walk-by visitors will recall the names or stories of any particular dissidents, they will surely at least remember that those artists and writers and activists exist and that—at least for some, especially some dictators—art has consequences. In the end, *@Large* was a blunt litany of injustice, a kind of wall of the missing.

Meanwhile, while we were wandering the halls of Alcatraz, another litany was being recited. Partway through the day, Twitter started lighting up with praise for President Obama and his speech at the base of the Edmund Pettus Bridge in Selma, Alabama. The president, along with members of Congress and hundreds of other dignitaries, was commemorating the fiftieth anniversary of Bloody Sunday and the march to demand voting rights in Alabama and across the South. Leaning on the words of James Baldwin and Walt Whitman, President Obama placed the Selma marchers at the center of the American character. Along with the Tuskegee Airmen and Navajo code talkers and police officers and firefighters, the president invoked "storytellers, writers, poets, and artists who abhor unfairness, and despise hypocrisy, and give voice to the voiceless, and tell truths that need to be told."

It was an inspirational speech, a nuanced speech, one in which the president not only celebrated the past but maintained a realistic view of the present. He decried ongoing racial injustice while acknowledging how far we've come. It was soaring and beautifully delivered. It reminded me of the candidate Barack Obama, with his aspirational rhetoric and eye on the meta-narrative. And yet, as much as it brought tears to my eyes to see Congressman John Lewis—who was beaten near to death that Sunday in 1965—jump up to embrace the nation's first African American president, I couldn't join in the applause wholeheartedly. I couldn't throw off my skepticism and alarm. Because while President Obama was celebrating the leavening function of artists and writers in a free society, he was also overseeing the largest program of mass surveillance the world has ever known. We know that his White House is letting—if not encouraging—the National Security Agency and who knows who else scoop up whatever information they can about whomever they can, sometimes with the rubber stamp of the Foreign Intelligence Surveillance Act (FISA) court, sometimes without. We know that the administration is cozy with Facebook and Google and Yahoo, all of which harvest private, soul-baring information about virtually every adult (and many children) on the planet, whether through individuals' own online activities or through tools like Google Maps, cell phone trackers, and widespread surveillance cameras.

I fear that while the president is out singing the praises of protest and dissent, he is simultaneously building and maintaining the infrastructure for totalitarianism. If I am honest with myself, I actually don't care that much if Barack Obama is perusing my Google searches, reading my texts with my children, tracking my car as it passes through tollbooths, or viewing my street day by day, but I sure don't want Ted Cruz or Scott

Walker doing it. And those two are certainly not the worst I can imagine. We know—Ai Weiwei and others have shown us—that the road from surveillance to harassment to arrest to torture to death is a well-worn path. And it is a tremendously tempting path for the powerful and even more so for would-be tyrants.

It would be easy to settle on "hypocritical" as the last word for President Obama as he both celebrates and violates civil liberties. And yet that isn't quite right, either. In 2009, when President Obama met with civil rights lawyers who were concerned about preventive detention, he is reported to have replied, "We have different roles. You represent clients and you are doing exactly what you should do. I am the president of the United States, with the responsibility to protect the American people. Do we just release them and take the chance they blow you up? There's only so much a democracy can bear."

So when the president beckons artists to "tell the truths that need to be told," perhaps he is not just papering over his own culpability but is calling artists to embrace their role in a pluralistic society. Perhaps he is drawing our eyes toward the work of Ai Weiwei and those activists Ai is commemorating and celebrating in *@Large*. Perhaps the president is issuing a challenge to the half million people who walked through a notorious American prison and saw the faces of world citizens suffering detention and torture. Perhaps, when President Obama reminds us that there are other bridges still to be crossed, he is provoking us to raise our voices in protest, to hold him accountable. Or maybe I just want to believe that if Barack Obama were not the president of the United States, he would be sounding the alarm, warning us of creeping authoritarianism.

Ai Weiwei conceives of the role of artists slightly differently than President Obama. While Ai embraces activism, he also elevates the promise of the artist's innermost sensibility: "Today the whole world is still struggling for freedom. . . . In such a situation, only art can reveal the deep inner voice of every individual with no concern for political borders, nationality, race, or religion." As a whole, *@Large* only partially fulfilled Ai's own vision. There were mere glimpses of the inner life, of the deep interiority that allows the viewer to sidle up to the consciousness of the artist. But on the other hand, *@Large* did fulfill the externalized civic role that President Obama imagines for art. A Chinese dissident on house arrest reached across the ocean and—with the assistance of the U.S. National Park Service—challenged the leaders of the world. Though *@Large* was neither subtle nor entirely clearheaded, it sounded the call and demanded that we pay attention.

July 2015

Article II, Section 1

Capturing the President

The executive power shall be vested in a President of the United States of America.

— Constitution of the United States
Article II, Section 1

I.

The Saucer That Cools the Cup
I spent the better part of yesterday afternoon poring over former White House photographer Pete Souza's gigantic and expensive new coffee-table book, *Obama: An Intimate Portrait*. It was a guilty pleasure, for sure, and perhaps one that wasn't great for my mental

health. The first photograph in the book is dated January 5, 2005, and captures newly sworn-in Senator Barack Obama sitting at a desk in a plain white room institutionally illuminated by panels of overhead fluorescent lights—no jacket, feet propped up next to a half-drunk bottle of water, flipping through the pages of a memo. A fat red book on the desk captures the eye. If you strain, you can read the title—*Master of the Senate,* the third volume in Robert Caro's definitive and seemingly endless biography of President Lyndon Johnson. That book is where Caro tells the possibly apocryphal story about Washington explaining to Jefferson the reason for having a two-house legislative system: "We pour House legislation into the senatorial saucer to cool it."

The final photograph in Souza's book was taken at 12:46 p.m. on January 20, 2017. It shows former President Obama in profile looking out over the White House from the helicopter Executive One. "We used to live there," Obama says.

The book is nearly 350 pages long and costs $50 to own, but I devoured it in one sitting. It left me feeling shaky and weepy and nostalgic for who we used to have in the White House and perhaps even more for what we thought we were as a country. There is a stomach-dropping picture in the last section of the book of the president talking to the White House communications team on the afternoon of November 9, 2016. The staff is in a semicircle around the president; the vice president is standing just to the left of him. There is not one smile in the room. Most everyone is standing with their heads tilted down or their arms folded across their chests. In a word, everybody looks sick.

For sure the contrast between what we had and what we have now could not be more stark. It is hard not to panic as I look at images of President Obama seriously, purposefully taking on the presidency, getting grayer and thinner with each frame; and then consider the chaos and cravenness that has taken over those same rooms, those same responsibilities.

Of course, there is also no doubt that the Obama family is ridiculously photogenic. The president always looks like the coolest guy in the room.

But there is more to it than impeccably framed nostalgia and good looks. There is something moving and unsettling about the proximity of the camera and the intimacy of the eye behind it. Pete Souza, who had first covered Obama for the *Chicago Tribune*, took the White House photographer job on the condition that he would have access to everything. The president agreed. As Obama says in the foreword: "Over the course of eight years in the White House, I probably spent more time with Pete Souza than with anybody other than my family."

Seeing all these photos together at such close range makes the presidency itself feel so monstrous, so impossible. Barack and Michelle Obama—and their daughters, Malia and Sasha— seem like regular people. They seem like decent, moral, hard-working Americans. They seem like people I could be friends with. But the presidency requires something else. As we are repeatedly told—the president of the United States is the most powerful person in the world. And the self-same President Johnson put it into perspective: "The presidency has made every man who occupied it, no matter how small, bigger than he was; and no matter how big, not big enough for its demands." The president has to make life-or-death decisions every single day while also serving as the moral compass for the country and the consoler in chief, regardless of his innate capacity or whether he just had a fight with his wife or whether he is battling the stomach flu. No one could possibly be up to the task.

In the spring of 2013, I was asked by the editors of *Poetry Northwest* to write an essay about the intersection of photography and poetry. I—along with the other writers in the issue—was allowed to choose any photo I liked. I chose a series of photos by Pete Souza, having no idea of what was to come. But now I am glad to have done it, to have chronicled what it felt like to study those photos closely without the benefit of hindsight. Without nostalgia or the dread of foresight. And even then, the unattainability of the ideal set by the presidency was clear, but I was grateful to have Barack Obama there, giving it his best shot.

March 2018

II.

Not Where He Is

Within hours of announcing to a stunned world that a team of Navy SEALs had raided a compound in suburban Pakistan where they had located and executed the world's most notorious terrorist—Osama bin Laden—the White House released a photograph that quickly became the most-viewed image in Flickr history and that has become known as "The Situation Room Photo." It was taken by White House photographer Pete Souza during the raid on the bin Laden compound and was, in fact, not taken in the official Situation Room at all, but rather in a small anteroom next door. But the name stuck.

The photograph frames a spare white room designed to seat only seven, but now overflowing with some of the nation's most recognizable—and powerful—citizens. Immediately, the viewer picks out President Obama, Vice President Biden, Secretary of State Clinton. But on closer look—and with the help of White House watchers—we realize the gathering also includes the chair of the Joint Chiefs of Staff, the secretary of defense, the director of national intelligence, the White House chief of staff, and other national security officials, several of whom have become household faces simply because they were captured in that photo.

They are gathered around a table with the president, the vice president, the secretary of state, and a few others seated. The rest are in a scrum at the back of the room. Air Force Brigadier General Brad Webb has the only obviously padded seat at the table, the one in the center, the one that looks like the president should be sitting in it. It turns out that General Webb was alone in the room first and everyone else followed later, but in the photo it looks as if the president has ceded his seat to the only person in uniform. The whole gathering is focused intently on what we speculate must be a television or a computer screen outside the frame of the photograph. Their faces bristle with tension. Secretary of State Hillary Clinton has her hand over her mouth, her eyes open wide, a paper cup of coffee on the table in front of her. The president is leaning onto his thighs, jaw tight, eyes narrowed, chin raised. He looks smaller than his standing-up stature of six foot one, thinner and graver and more tired than we are used to seeing him.

The photograph immediately became the subject of analysis and speculation and parody and even the requisite conspiracy theory suggesting that it was faked for some indeterminate political gain. It was held up as demonstrating changing attitudes about race and gender. But mostly, it was just mesmerizing. As then counterterrorism adviser—now the newly confirmed CIA director—John Brennan described the scene: "It was probably one of the most anxiety-filled periods of time, I think, in the lives of the people who were assembled. The minutes passed like days."

Like many people, I posted the picture on Facebook; I studied it, face by face; I discussed it with my husband and friends; I wondered about the power of it. What was it about that photo that caused pundits and all the rest of us to immediately elevate it to the stature of icon? To refer to it alongside the photograph of Harry Truman grinning over the top of the newspaper that wrongly crowed "Dewey Defeats Truman"? What is it about that photo?

Besides the drama of the moment, besides the daring and the risk and the palace intrigue over whether or not to launch the operation, I think there might be something more humble, more human about the magnetism of the Situation Room photo. In an era of multibillion-dollar presidential campaigns and twenty-four-hour news machines, we are almost desperate to see real humanity in these people who seem so far from us but who affect our lives and our futures so profoundly. We see these folks—a lot—but typically in highly controlled, extroverted, and staged situations. We see them fully made up in the masks of power. But what of the warm-blooded, breathing humans behind the masks? The ones who must make decisions on imperfect information, who bear prejudices and sore throats and blind spots? The ones who haven't slept and are missing their daughters' basketball games? How do we see who is really there, representing us, struggling on our behalf? And here I focus on the president and those around him, but I suppose the same questions could be asked of professional athletes or movie stars or anyone who seems larger than life. We want some glimpse of the private ruminations of those oh-so-public figures.

This is, of course, not a new longing. Poets and painters—and later photographers—have always stared into the faces of presidents for clues about what lay behind the surface. Gilbert Stuart, who painted the famous Lansdowne portrait of George Washington, contradicted the almost universally held belief in Washington's temperance and unflappability, concluding after studying and painting his face that "all his features were indicative of the strongest and most ungovernable passions." Similarly, Walt Whitman often stood in the streets of Washington, D.C., waiting for Abraham Lincoln to pass, pining: "I see very plainly Abraham Lincoln's dark brown face with the deep-cut lines, the eyes, always to me with a deep latent sadness in the expression." But he also said of the sixteenth president: "None of the artists or pictures has caught the deep, though subtle and indirect expression of this man's face. There is something else there."

The raw materials of poetry are different. As Robert Pinsky has said about poetry, it is "a vocal imagining, ultimately social but essentially individual and inward." While poets are expected to surface the inner life and voice of an individual, photographers—particularly presidential photographers—are working within a fundamentally external medium. Nonetheless, it is the precipice between the inner and outer life that can make poems and photographs unforgettable. In the case of presidents, poets and photographers struggle to create an image that captures both the inner and outer worlds of a person with access to seemingly limitless power. When Pete Souza was assigned by the *Chicago Tribune* to cover Barack Obama's first year in the

Senate, Souza sensed that Obama might someday ascend to the presidency, so he looked to capture those moments we "would never see again." Moments that were private, that were ordinary, that were anonymous.

James Dickey enacted a public imagining of a private moment in his poem "The Strength of Fields," which he read at the inaugural celebration of his fellow Georgian, President Jimmy Carter. The poem dramatizes a scene where a man who bears a tremendous resemblance to Carter walks the fields near his hometown to gather himself in anticipation of taking on the burdens and responsibilities of great power. It starts here, with the man walking alone, but only for the moment:

> Moth-force a small town always has,
>
>   Given the night.
>
>   What field-forms can be,
>   Outlying the small civic-light decisions over
>   A man walking near home?
>   Men are not where he is
> Exactly now, but they are around him   around him like the strength
>
>   Of fields.

It is a private moment, an inward moment, but the poem and the moment end here: "My life belongs to the world. I will do what I can."

The January 2013 inauguration provided a parallel image of Barack Obama, again in a photograph by Pete Souza. After the president was officially inaugurated, he walked toward the tunnel that would take him back into the Capitol. But before he entered the tunnel, he stopped and turned around to face the throngs spread across the National Mall. Souza captured the moment when the president had stopped and fully turned back toward the mall, toward the nation. Behind him are his wife, his mother-in-law, and his daughters watching him watch the country. In his face we can detect both awe and humility. A faint, faint smile suggests gratitude or pleasure or victory. A private moment captured at the most public of events.

The inauguration poem by Dickey and the inauguration photo by Souza freeze presidents on the threshold. They register the tick in time just before—or after—ordinary men put on the mantle of power and the knapsack of history and become something else. They capture the moment when they shape-shift, the moment when one of our own transforms into the most powerful person in the world.

But if I had to choose, as iconic as the Souza inauguration photo is, I would wager that it is the Situation Room photo that will endure. While the inauguration photo is moving and intimate, the thing that is so extraordinary about the Situation Room photo is that it captures the president at his most presidential. And by that I do not mean the most distorted by the glamour of power. I mean, rather, at the time when we most need a president to rise to the impossible demands of the office.

In the Situation Room photo, the president is not on the threshold—he is not going or coming. No, he is fully in it—the presidency—in fact leaning into it, facing one of the gravest and riskiest operations in recent history, sending a group of his fellow citizens into harm's way, knowing someone is likely to die.

He is the furthest he will ever be from ordinary citizenship, yet the image also reveals the inner strains of an ordinary man.

All of it—the burden, the responsibility, the focus, even the slight whiff of thrill—is there in his face. He is both human and superhuman, a person—a person who looks skinny and tired and tense—wielding tremendous power. And the photograph so clearly shows the burdens that go with it. So, as we look at that photo over and over, it reflects back to us the risks and rewards of self-governance, the beauty and peril of letting mortals make decisions of life or death. And now—to paraphrase Edwin Stanton at the time of Lincoln's death—that moment that captures a man in front of a television, that single moment that depicts a man with the fate of the world on his shoulders, now that moment belongs to the ages.

March 2013

III.

Truth, Lord, but I have marr'd them; let my shame
  Go where it doth deserve.
And know you not, says Love, who bore the blame?
  My dear, then I will serve.
                    —GEORGE HERBERT, "Love (III)"

Blessed Are We Poor
In these days where wealth and power are becoming ever more concentrated, there is comfort in a metaphor attributed to Jesus:

"It is easier for a camel to go through the eye of a needle, than for a rich man to enter into the kingdom of God." Even though my relationship to Christianity is an idiosyncratic and ultimately superstitious one, there is something at least shallowly appealing about the fundamentally democratic idea that no matter what our station in life, we are all the same before God. In fact, maybe the poor and the dispossessed are in a better position than the rich and the powerful when it comes to the Almighty because, according to Matthew, Jesus went on to say, "But many that are first shall be last; and the last shall be first."

That notion of equality and humility before God is certainly at play in the 2011 photograph of the Obama family standing before the huge statue of Christ the Redeemer—in Portuguese, Christo Rodentor—that looms over Rio de Janeiro. The photograph—once again by White House photographer Pete Souza—was taken during the president's first state visit to Brazil, the evening following the day that President Obama ordered U.S. airstrikes in Libya. The Christo Rodentor is ninety-nine feet tall—just under ninety-three feet taller than the president—and weighs seven hundred tons. It is the fifth-largest statue of Jesus in the world and is a national icon of Brazilian Christianity.

The photograph—with the looming Christ, arms outstretched, white-lit in the fog—appears to capture a group of nameless mortals called to account before God. The people are backlit and faceless, separated from one another, each of them with their head tipped up toward the huge and impassive Christ. Certainly, it is a reminder of human smallness, of our mortal imperfections and frailties in the face of death, in the face of God. The photograph could be of any of us—the most or the least of us—called to account before an imposing deity.

And yet, the longer you look at the image, the clearer it is that there is more to it than that. Because even though the night is dark, the fog is thick, and the faces are unseen, the man standing in the center of the group staring down the glowing Christ is still distinctly recognizable as President Barack Obama.

We know, even in silhouette, the particularities of that slump, the lanky stance with both hands in the pockets, the outline of those ears. We sense, even in the dark and mist, that this is no ordinary accounting. We cannot help but think about the airstrikes in Libya ordered earlier in the day, the drone strikes pounding Pakistan, the hunger strikes at the U.S. Detention Center in Guantanamo Bay. We can't help but think about the decisions this small, shadowy man has made on our behalf. We cannot help but remember the words of President Lincoln's second inaugural address, again quoting Matthew: "The Almighty has His own purposes. 'Woe unto the world because of offenses! for it must needs be that offenses come; but woe to that man by whom the offense cometh!'"

So in this context, Pete Souza's eerie and beautiful and haunting photograph—though I may be struck by lightning for saying it—deepens the metaphor offered by Jesus. It makes us wonder if perhaps, in our not-so-humble Republic, self-governance dooms the mighty. Because while most of us can afford to at least rhetorically align ourselves with the meek, going about our private lives, rarely, if ever, making such grave decisions on behalf of others, the president does not enjoy such luxuries. Through our choices in the voting booth, we propel people like Abraham Lincoln and Barack Obama and those before and after toward the eye of the needle, where power and responsibility require them to make decisions that separate them from the rest of us. In the words of the poet George Herbert, we are asking them to bow their heads and reply, "My dear, then I will serve." Under the spell of the poem and the parable and the photo, we can wonder if perhaps *we* bestow both power and doom on these men. As President Obama said at his recent inauguration, he swore "an oath to God and country." Jesus' parable, George Herbert's poem, and Pete Souza's photograph call to mind a complex accounting before both.

March 2013

Peeping in the Crack Under the Goddamn Door

*One Citizen's Reflections on the Phenom
That Is* S-Town

LIKE PROBABLY EVERYBODY ELSE IN MY ZIP CODE AND zip codes that resemble mine, I spent half of Donald Trump's first hundred days trying to figure out what in g-d's name just happened. The media told us that Donald Trump had tapped into the festering anger of the rural white working class, which the likes of me and my friends had left behind and sneered at for far too long. So I did what West Coast liberals do: I read books about it. First, I dived into *Hillbilly Elegy* by the now ubiquitous J. D. Vance, followed closely by *Strangers in Their Own Land* by Berkeley sociologist Arlie Russell Hochschild. Despite the narrative glue of Vance's book and Hochschild's admirable determination to climb what she calls the "empathy wall," I still didn't feel a real connection to the white, mostly conservative,

Protestant southerners at the heart of those books and at the heart of cultural divide we have talked so much about over the past few months.

That is, until I started listening to *S-Town*. For those who have been living under a rock or on a silent retreat for the last few months, *S-Town* is the latest podcast from the powerhouse production teams at *Serial* and *This American Life*. The on-air voice and co-producer of the project is Brian Reed, a reporter who opened a 2012 email addressed to *This American Life* with the subject line "John B. McLemore Lives in Shit-Town, Alabama." And that, as they say, was it.

McLemore was trying to entice someone from *This American Life* to investigate a murder he heard about while eavesdropping on some of the young guys he hired to help him on his 148 acres in Bibb County, Alabama. To cut to the chase, there was no murder, but John B. turns out to be one of the world's great cranks:

> We ain't nothing but a nation of goddamn chicken shit, horse shit, tattletale, pissy-ass, whiny, fat, flabby, out-of-shape, Facebook-looking, damn twerkfest, peeking out the windows, and slipping around listening in on the cell phones, and spying in the peephole, and peeping in the crack under the goddamn door, and listening into the fucking sheetrock. You know, Mr. Putin, please show some fucking mercy. I mean come on, drop a fucking bomb, won't you?

With the promise of an unsolved murder and a cast of characters even Faulkner could not have dreamed up, Brian Reed decides to keep pursuing the story. Thus begins a five-year journey, which might not be over yet, but at least so far has culminated in a seven-episode podcast that became *S-Town*, which—as of last counting—has been downloaded more than forty million times.

Much has already been said about *S-Town*, and every day more photos and reactions are published as it continues to bounce its way around the culture. The most common adjective for *S-Town*, used by both producers and reviewers, is "novelistic." I can see that. It's long-form, scene-based, character-driven, laden with metaphor. It was released all at one time. The episodes are called "chapters." And it is crazy-making and addictive in the same way that the best novels are. I could not stop thinking about it. I was irritable with the real-life people at home and at work because I was fretting over the struggles of the residents of Woodstock, Alabama.

But as I listened, the book I was most reminded of was not Truman Capote's famous "nonfiction novel," *In Cold Blood*, which other reviewers have compared *S-Town* to, but rather C. D. Wright's crazy journalistic extended-poem-biography-elegy-memoir thing, *One with Others*. That book details the history of her friend and acerbic mentor—Margaret Kaelin McHugh—whom Wright calls "V." V is, at least on the surface, more heroic than John B. McLemore. The reason Wright knew her at all was that V was cast out by her husband—with whom she had seven children—after getting involved in a civil rights march from Memphis to Little Rock. She tells the story of the march and the exile in exquisite C. D. Wright fashion, but even more than that, she reveals the thwarted brilliance of a choleric and highly literate woman limited by circumstance.

Like Brian Reed, C. D. Wright conducted dozens of interviews, and also like Reed, she drops many of them into the poem wholesale, letting the reader "hear" the voices outright. And though Wright clearly adored V and though V had passed on several years before the book was written, Wright didn't sugarcoat V or her quirks. Here's an example:

> She woke up in a housebound rage, my friend V. Changed diapers. Played poker. Drank bourbon. Played duplicate bridge. Made casseroles, grape salad, macaroni and cheese. Played cards with the priest. Made an argument for school uniforms, but the parents were concerned the children would be indistinguishable. She was thinking: affordable, uniforms. You can distinguish them, she argued, by their shoes. It was a mind on fire, a body confined.

There were cockfights and divorces and racist ex-husbands and neighbors and various forms of liquor on the ironing board. V was idealistic and brilliant and messy and flawed. And cantankerous as all get-out. In short, she bore some distinct resemblances to John B. McLemore.

And while poems have the same whispered-in-your-ear quality of a podcast in earbuds, there are some clear differences between *One with Others* and *S-Town*—the most obvious being, of course, the live human voices that we hear in sometimes uninterrupted minutes-long segments in the podcast. There are the sighs, the labored breathing, the stops and starts, the ups and downs of John B.'s moods. There is also Reed's willingness to be at least somewhat transparent with his own emotions. On several occasions, he mentions his discomfort with the liberal use of the "n-word" being tossed around Bibb County. And Reed describes his decision to make his Facebook and Instagram accounts private on the urging of his then girlfriend, now wife, whom he reveals is African American. You can hear Reed's skepticism in follow-up questions and hear him laugh at John's jokes.

But one of the most memorable segments of *S-Town* comes during the phone call that Reed receives in the days—and apologies for the massive spoiler here—after McLemore's suicide. Reed—as humans do when they receive terrible news—stumbles ("Are you kidding me? Oh my gosh"), fights tears ("Oh my gosh . . . mmmm"), apologizes ("I'm sorry. I'm still trying to take all this in. I'm trying to follow what you are saying. . . . It's just so shocking"). He wonders who he is in the scheme of Mc-Lemore's life and receives a touching answer from the twenty-one-year-old wife of one of John B.'s friends and protégés ("I mean, if you wasn't anything to this, I wouldn't have called").

But more than anything else, there is proximity. Reed is—and by extension we are—right up in the most intimate and painful details of these people's lives. John B. called himself a "semi-homosexual," and in one of his most controversial decisions, Reed summarizes an off-the-record conversation about a romantic relationship between John B. and a local man.

That proximity—and the often uncomfortable intimacy it creates—is the source of some critique, particularly in a widely circulated and provocatively titled review in *Vox*: "S-Town is a stunning podcast. It probably shouldn't have been made." In addition to the ethical gray area around revealing an off-the-record conversation about the romantic struggles of a gay man who kills himself in rural Alabama, the final chapter of *S-Town* is deeply unsettling and unforgettable, both because of the shocking nature of the content itself and because of the inherent voyeurism involved in witnessing the emotional breakdown of another human. Some of the most disturbing aspects come in the recollections of Tyler Goodson, whom John treats as a sort of adopted son. Goodson talks about what he and John B. came to call "church," a pain ritual that involved repeated tattoos (sometimes without ink) and almost daily nipple piercing that John B. begged for right up to the last hours of his life. It was, in the assessment of Reed, an elaborate form of cutting. It is extremely difficult to listen to. It is horrifying and grotesque and in many, many ways too close for comfort.

But, if I'm being honest, that segment was also tremendously enlightening about just how much John B. was suffering. I—along with most of America and part of the rest of the world—listened to John B. rant about impending doom and the horrors and indignities of Shit-Town. I heard him say that he was depressed and even that he planned to kill himself. But I really didn't feel the down-to-the-core suffering of John B. McLemore until I heard about church. It reveals in graphic, physical detail the obliterating pain behind the bombastic rants. And suddenly everything that John B. was comes into sharper focus.

Truth is, I'm not sure about the journalistic ethics or even the personal morality of revealing such intimate details about a man who can no longer consent to their airing. But for the first time, I really see the trade-offs between privacy and honest-to-god-up-close empathy. Up to now, I've been pretty strident in the privacy department. My favorite amendment is the Fifth—the one that gives us the right not to incriminate ourselves. My personal motto is "It's none of your business." I am a card-carrying member of the ACLU and class-A Ed Snowden fangirl.

And yet, in my unquestioned devotion to privacy, I didn't really think about the trade-offs between privacy and empathy.

I didn't really consider the cost of privacy in terms of our willingness to show up whole in the view of others. I didn't think about the fact that, by privileging privacy and personal autonomy above all else, we are somehow depriving ourselves of the opportunity to understand and be understood by one another.

The difference between the profiles that Arlie Hochschild presents in *Strangers* and Brian Reed unspools in *S-Town* comes in their intimacy and, frankly, in the transgressing of what we would ordinarily consider to be the interview subjects' privacy. Like Reed, Hochschild also did dozens of interviews over many years, going to church and McDonald's and riding around in trucks with her subjects in an effort to understand Tea Party activists—or at least sympathizers—in rural Louisiana. But in her case, there was a kind of polite distance between her and her subjects. Interviewees put their best foot forward: kind, competent, responsible, churchgoing, freedom-loving. We learn about illnesses most likely caused by chemical contamination and about the loss of beloved homes and habitat, but even suffering occurs at a presentable and socially acceptable arm's length. Not so with John B. McLemore and his friends (and enemies) in *S-Town*.

In a study of the Boston Marathon bombing published in the *European Physical Journal of Data Science*, Yu-Ru Lin and Drew Margolin conclude that people's willingness to "extend social support to those in need" is proportional to their physical and emotional proximity. Close proximity is directly related to whether people believe the tragedy affects "us" or whether it affects "others."

And, for all my squeamishness, that's what *S-Town* gives us—close and sometimes exquisitely uncomfortable proximity, making it impossible to see John B. and the others as alien or outside our sphere of care. Oddly, by risking the privacy of

John B. and Tyler and the lot of them so completely, Reed actually transcends what might have been a kind of exoticism. By going deeper and longer and closer, Reed makes it much more possible for the listener to see John B. McLemore as a complete and extremely complex person rather than an odd and entertaining but unknowable other.

The one last qualm I have about *S-Town*—and it is a big one—is the scale. Ten million people downloaded it in the first four days. That number has quadrupled, and the downloads continue as word spreads. *One with Others*—which also brought us close enough to scrutinize the very real frailties of a deceased iconoclast—will reach only a tiny fraction of that number, even though it was widely reviewed and fêted. To use myself as an example, I live twenty-six hundred miles from Woodstock, Alabama, and yet I have had several detailed conversations about whether John B. was suffering from mercury poisoning and about whether Tyler has completely compromised his criminal case because of how much he runs off his mouth. I can't help but think about all the other conversations all over the world dissecting the lives of these poor people.

I am reminded a bit of an article I read last fall called "Loved to Death: How Instagram Is Destroying Our Natural Wonders." The writer tells the story of a swimming hole here in Oregon that she and her family have visited for decades but now has hundreds of people descending on it every weekend because of idyllic pictures posted on social media. Apparently, this is a problem in wild areas across the world.

Like tens of millions of my closest friends, I felt like Brian Reed was whispering through my headphones just to me. Because of the proximity, the intimacy, the sensitivity of the story, it felt like it belonged to me or at least to a small group within the sound of his voice. But then there were sixteen million and then thirty million and then forty million other listeners. And they—like me—looked up pictures of John and Tyler and the house where John B. and his eighty-nine-year-old mother, Mary Grace, lived. So, though the relationship between John B. and Brian Reed was a personal and empathetic one, it became one that is now shared by a measurable percentage of the population of the United States. And that scale could not have been conceivable when John B. took up his late-night calls with Reed.

None of this is easy. Or ethically clear. But it is emotionally moving in a way that I haven't felt in a long time. One of the things a large and pluralistic society denies us is proximity to people who are unlike us. And with that denial, the lives of our fellow citizens are harder to imagine, creating a kind of empathetic poverty that erodes our shared life. Literature—of course—has always been one of the reliable bridges between us, and maybe the intimacy and proximity of *S-Town* is just a vivid twenty-first-century reminder of that truism. But I know that my relationship—such that it is—with John B. piques my curiosity about the man at the end of my block who keeps to himself and even the scowling Trump supporter raising his fist at a MAGA rally in Wisconsin. I am not ready to make proclamations about the ethics of privacy or the primacy of empathy, but I do know I am grateful to have known a bit about the beautiful and painful and tumultuous life of John B. McLemore. I know I am softer and more curious and more empathetic for it. Truth is, I am a better American for it.

June 2017

The Perfume of Resistance

*A Talk Given at the Association of
Writers & Writing Programs*

THESE DAYS, I'M LIVING WITH TWIN ANXIETIES. THE first is civic. I am terrified by what we have learned about mass government and corporate surveillance, about the erosion of our civil liberties, about the increasing infrastructure of authoritarianism. And we all have good reason to be afraid. Just yesterday, we learned that not only has the government been using blanket suspicionless surveillance in the name of national security, in the name of keeping us safe from terrorism, but that government investigators also have been using widespread data collection routinely in regular, mundane, day-to-day drug enforcement. And they've been using it since before 9/11.

My other fear, though, is more personal, more interior. I find myself worried about the state of my own imagination. I think I am becoming a little fuzzy around the edges. Not only is my ability to concentrate compromised by the velocity of twenty-first-century life—often a sustained argument or even a detailed metaphor feels like it is on the other side of a high, smooth wall—but I am growing suspicious of the contents of my own mind. I wonder about the source of my own interests, about why I find certain images or ideas or metaphors compelling, about why an obsession arises at a particular time.

And here's the thing, I suspect that these two anxieties—one public, one private—are not unrelated. I worry that some all-encompassing algorithm is not only reporting every detail of my outer life to Larry Page at Google and Michael Rogers at the NSA but is spitting back to me carefully curated data that is clotting my inner life as well.

Let me be clear. I love the internet. I love it mostly because I love research. It is one of life's great pleasures. I don't start a poem until I've compiled pages—sometimes dozens of pages—of notes and fragments and stray facts. I just wrote a poem that combined research about nineteenth-century Cincinnati, Wagner's opera *Tristan und Isolde*, and the native plants of the Black Forest in southern Germany. I'm certain I'm not alone when I say that the internet gives me a buzz like nothing else. I love the fact that I can follow a four-lane highway until I get to wagon ruts that give way to a goat path and then a mouse trail and then flattened grass; pretty soon, I have burrowed my way into a prairie dog hole.

There's that happy warmth that floods my system each time I make a new discovery. And I want more of it. But this is not exactly the Dewey Decimal System at the public library. While it feels like I have bumped into a goat path on a trek of my own making, these paths are not self-made and not necessarily benign. They are not worn into the rock by mammals who have spent centuries avoiding crevasses and perilous cliffs. No. They are paths bought and paid for by shadowy entities who want us to follow them to their company, their university, their cause. The paths are cleared and paved by algorithms based on what the hive mind has decided we must be looking for. The internet genies are tapping into our yearnings and are giving us dopamine shots along the way like bread crumbs on the trail. And each time we're lured down another brushy path, we clear it for the next person. And it's not just research for our poems and stories. It's our debit cards and GPS maps and tweets and friends on Facebook. It's our searches for orange ballet flats and for the most effective juice cleanses. Our individual interests and idiosyncrasies have become part of a massive sorting algorithm that boomerangs right back at us.

I guess I need to ask now, So what's the problem? What does it matter if my singular imagination merges with that of millions of others? If it becomes one data point among many in a massive crowdsourced culture? After all, as we learned in James Surowiecki's important book *The Wisdom of Crowds*, a crowd is better than an individual at guessing the weight of an ox. Why shouldn't we tap into that collective wisdom as we prepare to write our poems?

And some poets do. Some of the most skillful and talked-about recent poems mimic the fragmentary jump cuts and mass confusion of the culture. And we nod with recognition when we read them and hear them. But here's the thing: I actually don't need to be shown what the culture does to my imagination. I already live it.

What I need—as a reader and citizen—is a glimpse into

an intact consciousness. I need to live in another's skin for a moment, struggle inside their struggles, suffer unforgettable particularities that are similar—or dissimilar—to my own. That connection to the inner life of another is the wellspring of empathy—for myself, for my family, for those in the next town, for those in countries across the world.

Poems that grow from the deep space of an empathetic and capacious imagination bring us metaphor and meaning that provide a counterweight to that which is cynical and brutal. I can't help but think of the sophisticated online marketing done by ISIS, offering Middle Eastern and Western youth alike a pathway to certainty and connection and purpose. And how, despite scientific agreement that our fossil fuel use is incinerating the planet, we continue to consume it in ever vaster quantities. These problems we face seem urgent and alarming, so we throw policy solutions and negotiating teams at them. Good. I'm glad somebody is paying attention and is writing policy. But in some sense, these seething global forces seem to have archetypal roots—a search for meaning and a fear of death—and policy proposals don't speak archetype.

But archetypes and their corresponding metaphors and symbols are artists' stock-in-trade. I can't stop thinking about the temple that David Best and Helen Marriage built in Londonderry—or Derry as the Catholics call it—in Northern Ireland last month. Best, of Burning Man fame, worked with Catholic and Protestant kids to build an ornate wooden temple on a hill. Then—beyond all expectations—sixty thousand people visited the temple, many of whom had been directly affected by violence between Catholics and Protestants. They left photographs and locks of hair and prayers for reconciliation. And then, on the night of March 21, they set the temple on fire in a spectacular conflagration. That, my friends, is metaphor at work in the world. That is what Lawrence Ferlinghetti was urging on in poets when he said, "If you would be a poet, create works capable of answering the challenge of apocalyptic times, even if this means sounding apocalyptic."

We poets like to think we are witnesses to the maladies of our era. And we are. But we are also confined to the infirmary alongside everyone else. We are exposed to the same pathogens as the rest of the country, and it behooves us to do what we can to heal ourselves. Speaking of Ferlinghetti, his comrade Allen Ginsberg's great American poem "Howl" warned of the corporatized threat to the fragile, the marginalized, the expressive. Listen up here:

> What sphinx of cement and aluminum bashed open their
> skulls and ate up their brains and imagination?

> Moloch! Solitude! Filth! Ugliness? Ashcans and unobtain-
> able dollars! Children screaming under the stairways!
> Boys sobbing in armies! Old men weeping in the parks!

One thing Ginsberg, in all his fabulous naïve excess, reminds us of is that we live in a body—we are a body—and that the body can ground us and inoculate us, at least to some extent, against the colonization of the mind. So how about this? Let's stop eating out of cans and boxes and plastic wrap. I say this not to be high-handed and pure, but to remind us that food manufacturers are central players in the massive marketplace of yearning and satisfaction. Manufactured food is filled with salt and sugar and fat, making us always crave more and obliterating our taste buds against the subtler flavors that come from the ground and the sea. Let's run, jump, do burpees. Feel our feet and knees and heaving breath. Get out of our heads. Disrupt the hegemony of the mind and its pursuit of that which can be bought and sold. Meditate, practice yoga. Touch the ground. Plant a carrot, rake leaves, do the laundry. Eat dirt. Shovel manure. Whatever we can to bring ourselves back to our animal bodies.

Of course, we cannot become monks or pious refuseniks. We can't shut the door and turn our back on the suffering of other humans and creatures. But in our quest to keep up with the latest news, the latest horrors, we must be selective, self-critical, aware, not so certain all the time. We must maintain contact with the unconscious, the unseen world, the deep pool of intuition that is untouched by market forces and the shiny hope of a new pair of shoes. I do think it is our imperative to heal and protect our imaginations. Each and every one of us. If we don't, our capacity for right action and moral reckoning will become co-opted and maimed.

But that said, we also know that this is *not* only a problem of individual action. My laying off the Pringles and doing my daily walk around the park with the dog will not stop the forces that subsume and obliterate individual consciousnesses. No. As with so many other ills we face, we are confronted with massive power imbalances. One middle-aged lady poet versus the corporatized forces of capitalism combined with the full power of government is an unfair fight. The odds are stacked against me, against all of us. Big corporations know that our inner lives are valuable to them. Our yearnings and desires are essential to those who would sell us satisfaction. And our inner lives are also irresistible to the government. By examining whom we are associating with, where we are going, what we are reading and searching and watching, the government can detect the seed of a dangerous idea before it becomes dangerous or even really becomes an idea. And we know where that leads.

We know them by name—Václav Havel, Nelson Mandela, Martin Luther King Jr., Angela Davis. Even as we sit here today, Saudi Arabian blogger Raif Badawi faces a sentence of one thousand lashes for "insulting Islam." Writer and activist Chen Wei remains in prison in China for essays critical of the state. And Egyptian poet Shaimaa al-Sabbagh was shot in the street by the police as she carried a wreath of flowers to commemorate the uprising in Tahrir Square.

We cannot be cozy in believing that these are the problems of other countries, of other times. American filmmaker Laura Poitras lives in Berlin because she has been detained and searched by U.S. law enforcement so many times she is afraid her footage will be confiscated. And Edward Snowden is in what appears to be permanent exile for revealing the scope and breadth of NSA spying.

A recent poll of American writers and journalists conducted by PEN America found that a majority of writers assume that *all* of their communications are monitored by the government. Let me say that again, a majority of writers assume *all* of their communications are monitored. And as a result, almost 17 percent of writers have avoided speaking or writing about a particular topic. And another 10 percent have seriously considered it. That means more than a quarter of all writers and artists may not put their work into the world because of fear of government surveillance. That is nothing short of a crisis of the imagination.

This makes me think of our obligations as writers a little differently. What if we worked together to resist the creep of massive, toxic culture? What if we didn't merely look to one another as resources to learn craft and build networks but also bolstered one another's efforts to protect our individual imaginations and fostered support for writers in harm's way? What if we fomented collective opposition to corporate and government intrusion into our communications, into our very minds? What if—together—we became a bulwark against the forces that pry into our inner lives for their own purposes?

Let us go forth once again in the company of Lawrence Ferlinghetti:

> [Poetry] is the incomparable lyric intelligence brought to bear upon fifty-seven varieties of experience.

> It is the energy of the soul, if soul exists.

> It is a high house echoing with all the voices that ever said anything crazy or wonderful.

> It is a subversive raid upon the forgotten language of the collective unconscious.

> Poetry is a life-giving weapon deployed in the killing fields.

> Poetry is the perfume of resistance.

March 2015

ACKNOWLEDGMENTS

———————————

MANY THANKS TO THE EDITORS OF THE FOLLOWING publications in which these essays first appeared. Some of them first appeared in slightly different forms or under different titles.

Oregon Humanities
Are We Here?: *Fretting Over the Future of the Republic in the Garden of the West*
The Rim of the Wound: *An Open Letter to the Students of Columbia University's Multicultural Affairs Advisory Board, with a Special Note to My Own Daughters*
Where the World I Know and the World I Fear Threaten to Meet

The Los Angeles Review of Books
An All-or-Nothing Gamble: *Václav Havel and His Spiritual Revolution*

New England Review
These Are Strange Times, My Dear: *Considering Ai Weiwei's* @Large

NER Digital
The Word Made Flesh: *On Encountering the Work of Marcel Broodthaers*

The Rumpus
I Hear the Place That Can't Be Named: *One Writer's Reflections on the Right to Be Forgotten*
Reckoning with the Bros: *Donald Trump, Robert Bly, and Swimming in the Sea of Grief*
Peeping in the Crack Under the Goddamn Door: *One Citizen's Reflections on the Phenom That Is S-Town*
The Perfume of Resistance: *A Talk Given at the Association of Writers & Writing Programs*

Zócalo Public Square
The Sacred and Profane of Vote-by-Mail
I'd Have to Cry These Wounds to Mourn for Us

Poetry Northwest
Not Where He Is: *Capturing the President*
Blessed Are We Poor

A Million People on One String: *Big Data and the Poetic Imagination*

TREMENDOUS THANKS TO ANN PANCAKE AND WHITNEY Otto and all my friends and comrades in Workshop 8 who read drafts of this book. A big fat hat tip to Neisha Saxena, who gave me the title "A Gnostic Bill of Rights." Thank you to Jack Shoemaker for making this an infinitely better book. And to all the others at Counterpoint, who approach book-making with bottomless smarts and good cheer. Of course, all the gratitude to Ruby and Violet for loving fiercely and inspiring me to be better. And thanks to Lucas, who is an extraordinary and hilarious conversationalist. So many of these essays started around the dining room table at home. And to David, for bringing brilliance and heart to every single day.

WENDY WILLIS is a writer living in Portland, Oregon. Winner of the Dorothy Brunsman Poetry Prize, she has published two books of poetry. Willis is a lawyer, the executive director of the Deliberative Democracy Consortium, and the founder and director of Oregon's Kitchen Table at Portland State University. She also writes at twowomenandarepublic.com.